Business Result

SECOND EDITION

Pre-intermediate *Teacher's Book*

Rachel Appleby,
Mark Bartram
& David Grant

Great Clarendon Street, Oxford, OX2 6DP, United Kingdom

Oxford University Press is a department of the University of Oxford.
It furthers the University's objective of excellence in research, scholarship,
and education by publishing worldwide. Oxford is a registered trade
mark of Oxford University Press in the UK and in certain other countries

ISBN: 978 0 19 473882 8   Book
ISBN: 978 0 19 473881 1   Pack

Printed in China

This book is printed on paper from certified and well-managed sources

ACKNOWLEDGEMENTS

Cover image: Getty Images/Maya

Back cover photograph: Oxford University Press building/David Fisher

Contents

Introduction

The course

Who is *Business Result Second Edition* for?

Business Result Second Edition is a comprehensive multi-level course in business English suitable for a wide range of learners. The main emphasis is on *enabling* your students; helping them to communicate more effectively in their working lives.

In-work students

Unlike many business English courses, *Business Result Second Edition* addresses the language and communication needs of employees at all levels of an organization, who need to use English at work. It recognizes that the business world is truly international and that many people working in a modern, global environment spend much of their time doing everyday tasks in English – communicating with colleagues and work contacts by phone, via email and in a range of face-to-face situations, such as formal and informal meetings/discussions, and various planned and unplanned social encounters. It contains topics and activities that allow the students to participate in a way that is relevant to them, whatever their level in their company or organization.

Pre-work learners

Business Result Second Edition can also be used with pre-work learners at college level. The course covers a variety of engaging topics over the 15 units, so students without much work experience will receive a wide-ranging overview of the business world, as well as acquiring the key communication skills they will need in their future working lives. Each unit in this *Teacher's Book* contains suggestions for adapting the material to the needs of these students.

One-to-one teaching

Many of the activities in the book are designed for use with groups of students, but they can also be easily adapted to suit a one-to-one teaching situation. Notes in the individual *Teacher's Book* units offer suggestions and help with this.

What approach does *Business Result Second Edition* take?

Business Result Second Edition helps students communicate in English in real-life work situations. The priority at all times is on enabling them to do so more effectively and with confidence. The target language in each unit has been carefully selected to ensure that students will be equipped with genuinely useful, transferable language that they can take out of the classroom and use immediately in the workplace.

The course recognizes that, with so many businesses now being staffed by people of different nationalities, there is an increasing trend towards using English as the language of internal communication in many organizations. As well as learning appropriate language for communicating externally – with clients or suppliers, for example – students are also given the opportunity to practise in situations that take place within an organization, such as giving a report, making arrangements and taking part in meetings.

The main emphasis of the course is on the students speaking and trying out the target language in meaningful and authentic ways; it is expected that a large proportion of the lesson time will be spent on activating students' interest and encouraging them to talk. The material intentionally takes a communicative, heads-up approach, maximizing the amount of classroom time available to focus on and practise the target language. However, you will also find that there is plenty of support in terms of reference notes, written practice and review material.

The syllabus is essentially communication-driven. The topics in each of the 15 units have been chosen because of their relevance to modern business and the world of work. Vocabulary is presented in realistic contexts with reference to real companies or organizations. Grammar is also a key element of each unit. It is presented in an authentic context and ensures that students pay attention to accuracy, as well as become more proficient at expressing themselves clearly and precisely. The *Business communication* sections ensure that students are provided with a range of key expressions they can use immediately, both in the classroom and in their day-to-day work.

STUDENT'S BOOK

The *Student's Book* pack

The *Student's Book* pack offers a blend of classroom teaching and self-study, with an emphasis on flexibility and time-efficiency. Each of the fifteen *Student's Book* units provides around four hours of classroom material with the potential for two to three hours of additional study using other materials in the pack.

The materials that support the *Student's Book* units are:
- *Viewpoint* video lessons
- Practice files
- Progress tests
- Photocopiable worksheets
- *Online practice*

More information on all of these materials and how to use them can be found later in these Introduction pages.

Key features of a unit

Starting point

Each unit opens with some lead-in questions to raise awareness of, and interest in, the unit theme. Use these questions to help you establish what students already know about the topic and how it relates to their own working lives. These questions can usually be discussed as a class or in small groups.

Working with words

This first main section introduces key vocabulary in a variety of ways, including authentic reading texts, listening texts and visuals. Students are also encouraged to look at how different forms of words (verbs, adjectives and nouns) can be built from the same root, or to look at common combinations (e.g. verb + noun, adjective + noun) that will help them to expand their personal lexicon more rapidly. This section also offers opportunities to work on your students' reading and listening skills.

Language at work

The grammar is looked at from a communicative point of view; this will meet your students' expectations with regard to learning form and meaning, but also reminds them how the grammar they need to learn commonly occurs in business and work situations. The *Language point* highlights the target grammar structures, which are then practised in authentic work contexts.

Practically speaking

This section looks at various practical aspects of everyday communication and social interaction from a 'how to' perspective – for example, *How to avoid negative answers*, *How to ask for directions* – as well as useful ways that we use language in communication, such as *How to link ideas*.

Business communication

This section focuses on one of five broad communication themes – meetings, presenting, exchanging information, phone calls and socializing. These are treated differently throughout the book so that, for example, students are able to practise exchanging information on the phone as well as face-to-face, or compare the different language needed for giving formal and informal presentations. Typically, the section begins with students listening to an example situation (a meeting, a presentation, a social encounter, a series of phone calls). They focus on *Key expressions* used by the speakers which are listed on the page. They are then given the opportunity to practise these in various controlled and more open work-related tasks.

Tips

Throughout each unit, there are short, practical tips with useful language points arising from a particular section or exercise.

Talking point

All units end with a *Talking point*. These provide the opportunity for students to discuss a range of business concepts, approaches and ideas and how they might apply these in their own work. All of the topics relate to the unit theme and provide the opportunity for students to use the language from the unit.

The *Talking point* follows a three-part structure: Input (a short text, listening or infographic), Discussion, Task.

*Note that in some units the *Talking point* format is presented as a game. This is designed to be fun and is aimed at recycling the language from the unit.

Viewpoint

After every three units there is a two-page *Viewpoint* video lesson. The topic of the *Viewpoint* lesson relates to a theme from the preceding units and includes interviews and case studies of real companies. Each *Viewpoint* has a number of short videos and is divided into three or four sections. Each

lesson usually opens with an introduction to the topic and interviews with people discussing the topic. Key words and phrases are then introduced before students watch the main video section. Here, students can develop listening and note-taking skills with language presented in an authentic context. Each lesson ends with activities to give students speaking practice discussing the topic of the lesson.

Additional material

At the back of the *Student's Book*, you will find the following sections.

Practice files

These provide unit-by-unit support for your classroom work. Each file provides additional practice of target language from the three main unit sections, *Working with words*, *Language at work*, and *Business communication*. This can be used in two ways:

For extra practice in class – refer students to this section for more controlled practice of new vocabulary, grammar, or key expressions before moving to the next stage. The optimum point at which to do this is indicated by cross-references in the *Student's Book* unit and the teaching notes in this book.

For self-study – students can complete and self-check the exercises for review and revision outside class.

Answers for the *Practice file* exercises appear on pages 93–96 of this book.

Communication activities

Additional information for pairwork and group activities.

Audio scripts

Irregular verb list

TEACHER'S BOOK

What's in each unit?

Unit content

This provides an overview of the main aims and objectives of the unit.

Context

This section not only provides information on the teaching points covered in the unit, but also offers some background information on the main business theme of the unit and its importance in the current business world. If you are less familiar with the world of business, you will find this section especially helpful to read before starting a unit.

Teaching notes and answers

Notes on managing the *Student's Book* exercises and various activities are given throughout, with suggested variations that you might like to try. You will find comprehensive answers to all *Student's Book* exercises, as well as notes on possible responses to discussion questions.

One-to-one

In general, you will find that *Business Result Second Edition* can be used with any size of class. However, with one-to-one students you will find that activities which have been designed with groups of students in mind will need some adaptation. The *Teacher's Book* provides suggestions for how to adapt group work activities successfully for one-to-one classes.

Pre-work learners

Although most users of *Business Result Second Edition* will be students who are already in work, you may also be teaching classes of students who have little or no experience of the business world. The *Teacher's Book* provides suggestions for how to adapt certain questions or tasks in the book to their needs, and extra notes are given for these types of learners.

Extension

With some students it may be appropriate to extend an exercise in some way or relate the language point more specifically to a particular group of students. Suggestions on how to do this are given where appropriate.

Extra activity

If you have time or would like to develop further areas of language competence, extra activities are suggested where they naturally follow the order of activities in the *Student's Book*. For example, if your students need writing practice or need to build more confidence with speaking, extra follow-up ideas may be provided.

Alternative

With some students it may be preferable to approach an activity in a different way, depending on their level or their interests. These options are provided where appropriate.

Pronunciation

Tips on teaching pronunciation and helping students improve their intelligibility are provided where there is a logical need for them. These often appear where new vocabulary is taught, or for making key expressions sound more natural and fluent.

Dictionary skills

It's helpful to encourage students to use a good dictionary in class and the relevant notes suggest moments in the lesson when it may be useful to develop your students' skills in using dictionaries.

USING THE COURSE

How to use *Business Result Second Edition* to fit your teaching context

Business Result Second Edition provides all the flexibility you need as a teacher. The syllabus and content has been carefully designed so that it can be used either from start to finish or in a modular way, allowing you to tailor the course to suit your and your students' needs.

Using the course from start to finish

You can, of course, use *Business Result Second Edition* conventionally, starting at *Unit 1* and working your way through each unit in turn. If you do so, you will find it works well. Each section of the unit is related thematically to the others, and there is a degree of recycling and a steady progression towards overall competence, culminating in the *Talking point*. Timing will inevitably vary, but allow approximately four classroom hours for each unit. You will need more time if you intend to do the *Practice file* activities in class.

The 'flexible' option

Business Result Second Edition is written in a way that recognizes that many business English courses vary greatly in length. With this in mind, teachers can use *Business Result Second Edition* in a modular way. Although each unit has a logical progression, you will find that all the sections are essentially free-standing and can be used independently of the rest of the unit.

This modular approach provides the flexibility that business English teachers need when planning their course. Teachers might want to choose the sections or unit topics that are the most relevant and interesting to them and their students.

Online practice and teacher resources

For students

The *Online practice* gives your students additional language practice of the *Student's Book* content. For more information, see page 5 of the *Student's Book*.

For teachers

As well as providing access to all of the student online practice exercises, the Learning Management System (LMS) provides an invaluable and time-saving feature for teachers.

You can monitor your students' progress and all of their results at the touch of a button. You can also print off and use student reports on their progress.

A user manual for how to use the LMS can be found in the teacher resources in the *Online practice*.

Downloadable resources for teachers

In the teacher resources in the *Online practice* are a number of downloadable resources for teachers to use to complement the *Student's Book*. These include:

- Photocopiable worksheets for every unit
- Progress tests for every unit
- Business cards for role-plays
- Class audio
- Class video

Photocopiable worksheets

New for *Business Result Second Edition* are the photocopiable worksheets. These provide extra communicative practice, often in the form of a game, for every *Working with words*, *Language at work*, and *Business communication* section from the *Student's Book*.

There are suggestions in the *Teacher's Book* for when to use these worksheets in class. All of the worksheets, as well as the answer key, can be downloaded and photocopied from the teacher resources in the *Online practice*.

Photocopiable Progress tests

These can be administered at the end of each unit in order to assess your students' progress and allow you, the student or the head of training to keep track of students' overall ability.

Each test is divided into two sections. The first section tests the vocabulary, grammar and key expressions from the unit. This section is scored out of 30 and students will need about 30 minutes to complete the questions.

The second section is a speaking test. In this section students are given a speaking task that resembles one of the speaking activities in the unit. These are mostly set up as pairwork activities in the form of role-plays, discussions or presentations.

Marking criteria is provided to help you assess students' performance in the speaking test. It requires students to perform five functions in the speaking test, and you can grade each of the five stages using a scoring system of 0, 1 or 2, giving a final score out of 10.

The speaking test role-plays can also be used as extra classroom practice without necessarily making use of the marking criteria.

All of the tests, and the answer keys, can be downloaded from the teacher resources in the *Online practice*.

Business cards

There is a set of downloadable business cards in the teacher resources in the *Online practice*.

The business cards are particularly useful to use in role-play situations from the *Student's Book* if you have students from the same company and they are required to exchange information about their company. You will find suggestions of when to use the business cards in the teacher notes of the *Teacher's Book*.

Class audio and video

All of the class audio and the videos for the *Viewpoint* lessons can be streamed or downloaded from the teacher resources in the *Online practice*.

Alternatively, class audio can be played from the audio CD and the videos can be played from the DVD that is found in the *Teacher's Book* pack.

How to access the *Online practice*

For students

Students use the access card on the inside front cover of the *Student's Book*. This contains an access code to unlock the content in the *Online practice*.

For teachers

Teachers need to go to **www.oxfordlearn.com** and either register or sign in. Members of the Oxford Teacher's Club can use their existing sign in details.

Then click on **Register an organization** and follow the instructions. Note that if you are not part of an organization, or you don't have an authorization code from your institution, you will need to click on **Apply for an organization account**. You will then be asked to supply some information. If you don't have an institution, then put your own name next to Institution name.

Teacher's website

Additional teacher resources can be found at **www.oup.com/elt/teacher/businessresult**.

1 Companies

Unit content

By the end of this unit, students will be able to
- talk about what companies do
- talk about their company using the present simple
- ask somebody to repeat information
- introduce themselves and others.

Context

The topic of *Companies* gives the students the basic initial tools for business interaction. Anybody who works or plans to work in business will need a certain amount of vocabulary for describing a company, including its main activities, its location and its workforce. Not only is it important to find out about a contact's company for practical business reasons, but it is also a subject of interest to most business people, and so will be a topic of conversation in many business situations, including socializing.

Social interaction in business is crucial for the forging of good relationships and making new contacts. Cultural differences can lead to misunderstandings if business people do not use the appropriate expressions and intonation in their initial exchanges.

In this unit, students will learn how to describe their companies. They will also have the opportunity to practise two important social aspects of business interaction – asking people to repeat key information and introducing themselves and others. At the end of the unit, the students will play a game that will help them practise the language studied.

Starting point

Do the first question with the whole class. Give them cues if they are hesitant: Is it a big or small company? Is it an industrial or a service company? Is it local, national or international? The second question can be done with the whole class or in pairs before whole-class feedback. Encourage them to develop their answers.

PRE-WORK LEARNERS Ask learners what kind of company they would like to work for.

Working with words

Exercise 1

Allow students a few minutes to discuss the question in pairs, e.g. what products the companies make or services they provide, where they are based, how many people work for them, and how old the companies are.

Exercise 2

Students read the text and match the descriptions to the companies in **1**. Tell students it's not necessary to understand all the words, only the general sense. Provide feedback on answers with the whole class.

> **Answers**
> 1 Yahoo! 2 Michelin 3 Ikea 4 Ben and Jerry's
> 5 Samsung

Exercise 3

Students work in pairs to discuss the questions about the companies in **2**. Elicit some of their answers.

Exercise 4

Students complete the sentences with the words in bold from **2**. Do the first one together. When they have finished, ask them to compare in pairs before checking the answers with the group.

> **Answers**
> 1 produce   6 subsidiary
> 2 provide   7 operates
> 3 specialize   8 competitor
> 4 employee   9 exporter
> 5 based   10 revenue

Exercise 5

Refer students to the *Tip*, then ask them to count the syllables in each word in **4**. Do the first two together (*produce* and *provide*). Ask students to underline which syllable is stressed. If they aren't sure, say the words aloud for them and ask them which is correct, e.g. *Is it produce or produce?* Then ask them to do the same for the other words, encouraging them to say them aloud to see if the pronunciation sounds correct. Check answers with the whole class.

Answers

1 pro<u>du</u>ce (2 syllables)
2 pro<u>vide</u> (2)
3 <u>spe</u>cialize (3)
4 em<u>plo</u>yee (3)
5 <u>based</u> (1)
6 sub<u>si</u>diary (4 or 5)
7 <u>ope</u>rates (3)
8 com<u>pe</u>titor (4)
9 ex<u>por</u>ter (3)
10 <u>re</u>venue (3)

Exercise 6

As an introduction, ask students to close their books and tell you about the Volkswagen group, e.g. where their cars are made, the names of some of them, etc. You could ask them to do this in pairs before eliciting answers from the group.

Then ask students to open their books and complete the text, before checking answers with the whole class.

Answers

1 produces
2 subsidiary
3 based
4 operates
5 employees
6 competitors
7 specializes
8 provide

Further practice

If students need more practice, go to *Practice file 1* on page 106 of the *Student's Book*.

Exercise 7

Ask the students to discuss the question in pairs or small groups. What companies is their country famous for? Does it export to other countries? Encourage students to use some of the words from **4**.

Exercise 8

▶ 1.1 Give students time to study the table. Ask them what kind of information they need to listen for. Play the listening. They can then compare answers in pairs before listening a second time. Check their answers with the whole class.

Answers

1 locks
2 security systems
3 Eastern Company
4 Swedish
5 43
6 5
7 70
8 150
9 Besam

Exercise 9

Students work in pairs to make sentences. Encourage them to use words from **4**. Monitor and give feedback on good use of vocabulary and correct pronunciation (word stress).

Exercise 10

Students work in pairs with someone from another company, if possible. If students are all from the same

company, follow the suggestions in the *Pre-work learners* section below. You might like to provide a model first and ask students to guess the name of the company, e.g. *I work for X. We make cars. We have about 3,000 employees. We are based in Italy. Our main competitors are Porsche and Maserati. It's a subsidiary of Fiat. We specialize in sports cars, and we have sales of over €2.5 billion.* (Ferrari)

Give students time to prepare this speaking activity. Weaker students may want to write notes. To make it more challenging, you could ask the person listening to write notes on what their partner said. You could then ask two or three students to report back to the class from their notes.

PRE-WORK LEARNERS Ask students to imagine they work for a (real) well-known company. You could do this activity as a further practice exercise in the next lesson and ask them to research the necessary information (revenue, employees, etc.) online.

Photocopiable worksheet

Download and photocopy *Unit 1 Working with words worksheet* from the teacher resources in the *Online practice*.

Language at work

Exercise 1

Students ask and answer the questions in pairs. Make a note of three or four sentences that they say, of which at least one should be incorrect. You will use these sentences after **3**, to illustrate the language point.

PRE-WORK LEARNERS Ask students to think of a company they would like to work for, or one they have worked for in the past.

Exercise 2

Students read the statements and decide if they are true or false; ask them to correct the false sentences. Check the answers with the whole group.

Answers

1 T
2 T
3 F (It produces food.)
4 F (Only Toyota produces cars.)
5 T
6 T

Exercise 3

As this may be the first time they have done this type of grammatical analysis, you could guide the whole class through the activity rather than working in pairs.

Point out that all the verbs in **2** are in the present simple. Then refer them to 1–5 in the *Language point*, and ask them to find examples from **1** and **2** for each. Note that for some of the categories there is more than one example.

When you come to sentences a–c, they may not be familiar with the terms *second / third person* or may not be confident of the difference between an adjective and a verb. Be ready to give or elicit examples of these.

When you have finished, write the student sentences you noted from **1** on the board. Ask the students to find the incorrect sentence(s), and to correct them.

Answers
1 produces, provides, does (students may also list *is*)
2 Nestlé provides services but it doesn't produce anything; Nestlé and Gazprom don't have their head office in Japan.
3 The companies aren't competitors; Toyota isn't Russian.
4 Which company do you work for? What does it do? Do you work at the head office? Does the company have offices in other countries?
5 Is it a new company?
a facts or regular actions
b third
c be (questions with adjectives), do (questions with verbs)

Grammar reference
If students need more information, go to *Grammar reference* on page 107 of the *Student's Book*.

Exercise 4
Ask students to read the text. Elicit what kind of text it is (a website page giving information about a radio programme). You may need to explain the phrase *protect the environment*.

Ask students to choose the correct words in italics, referring to the grammar explanations in **3** where necessary. They should work individually, then compare their answers in pairs. Discuss answers as a class, eliciting why students' answers are not correct if they choose the wrong option.

Answers
1	know	7	do
2	produce/produces	8	talks
3	see	9	learns
4	do	10	are
5	does	11	don't
6	isn't		

Note that when talking about companies (or 'the police' or 'the staff'), we can use either a singular or plural verb.

Exercise 5
▶ **1.2** Play the listening once. Students listen for interesting facts. When they have compared answers in pairs, ask the whole class for two or three interesting facts that they heard.

Possible answers
Their first product was baby milk; Nestlé still produces baby products today; it has a huge number of factories; Nestlé provides a lot of training, etc.

Exercise 6
▶ **1.2** Ask students to read the questions and see how many they can answer from memory. Then play the listening again and give students time to compare answers in pairs before checking with the whole class. If necessary, play the listening again, pausing when the answer to each question is given, to give students more time to note their answers.

Answers
1 over 150 years old
2 baby products, food and drink products, chocolate and confectionery, bottled water, breakfast cereals, ice cream
3 90 billion Swiss francs
4 Vevey in Switzerland
5 447
6 over 300,000
7 Yes, it is (80% of employees do training courses).
8 Yes, it does (it gives money and other help).
9 Yes, it is (it uses less water, energy and packaging).

Exercise 7
Students use the information from **6** to make sentences about Nestlé. Stronger classes may be able to do this exercise orally. Weaker students should write the sentences and could do this exercise with a partner. As this is an accuracy exercise, you should insist on a fairly high level of grammatical precision, especially with the present simple verb forms. Suggest they try to write about 50 words.

Possible answers
It specializes in food and beverages. Its annual revenue is around 90 billion Swiss francs. Its head office is in Vevey, Switzerland. It has 447 factories. The company sells on all five continents. It employs over 300,000 people. 80% of employees do training courses. It gives money and other help to the community. It protects the environment by using less water, energy and packaging.

Further practice
If students need more practice, go to *Practice File 1* on page 107 of the *Student's Book*.

Exercise 8
Students work in pairs and ask and answer the questions from **6** about each other's companies or a company they know well. You may need to help with vocabulary, especially for questions 8 and 9, which may need vocabulary different from that of the listening text. Students should note down the answers in preparation for **9**.

Exercise 9
Put the students in new pairs. They should report to their new partner about the first partner's company. Make sure they use the third person forms correctly.

EXTENSION If you have a group with students from a range of companies, you could ask them to bring in some material next lesson to show each other and exchange information about their companies.

Photocopiable worksheet
Download and photocopy *Unit 1 Language at work worksheet* from the teacher resources in the *Online practice*.

Practically speaking

Exercise 1
Start by asking students why it's sometimes necessary to ask people to repeat something, e.g. because they speak too quickly or their accent is difficult to understand. Reassure them it's normal not to understand everything, and that asking for repetition is an important part of good communication. Then ask students to read the question, and elicit one or two answers from the class. Say which expressions are correct or incorrect but don't provide any new language for the moment.

Suggested answers
Sorry, can you repeat that / say that again? What's your name / the name of your company again? And where do you work?

Exercise 2
▶ **1.3** Explain that students are going to listen to somebody asking the speaker to repeat. Play the listening and ask students to compare their answers in pairs before checking their answers with the whole class.

Exercise 3

▶ **1.3** Before playing the listening again, ask students if they can remember any of the missing expressions. Then play it again, pausing the listening after each sentence and eliciting the missing words. Check the answers together.

Answers
1 say that again
2 speak, more slowly
3 how many
4 what are, again

Exercise 4

Students read the questions in **3** again and decide which ones ask the speaker to repeat only part of the information. Elicit answers from the whole class. For the second question, make sure they are using the correct rising intonation when they give the answers.

Answers
Questions 3 and 4 ask the speaker to repeat only part of the information.
Similar questions in response to the person in **1**: Sorry, what's your name (again)? Sorry, who do you work for (again)? / What's your company (again)? Where do you work (again)?

Refer students to the *Tip* and point out that it is important for your voice to go up in the second question because it shows you are asking the person to repeat something (and not just asking a stupid question that has already been answered!). Model the two questions in the *Tip* for the students, and ask them to repeat after you.

Exercise 5

Students work on their own and write down five facts about themselves or their company. Then ask them to choose one key word (a fact) in each sentence to cross out. You could demonstrate this yourself first, e.g. *I work for **** language school. I've been teaching for **** years. The school has offices on **** street. There are **** full-time teachers,* etc. Monitor and make sure the students respond using the target expressions in **3** and with the correct intonation.

Business communication

Exercise 1

Discuss the question briefly with the whole class.

Possible answers
Their nationality, where they live or work, their company, their job, why they are at the conference, if it's their first time, which talks or presentations they are going to, if they are going to present something, etc.

Exercise 2

▶ **1.4** Make sure students understand the phrase *introduce yourself*. Play the listening once only. Let students compare their answers in pairs and then check them with the group.

Answers
1 Argentinian
2 (self-employed) journalist
3 She's here to research an article (on Internet service providers).

EXTENSION Ask students to compare their ideas in **1** with what they heard in **2**. Were any of their ideas mentioned?

Exercise 3

▶ **1.4** Students read the conversation and try to complete it. Then play the listening for students to check. Let them compare answers in pairs. If necessary, listen again and pause after each gapped sentence to elicit the answer.

Answers
1	Is	6	why
2	introduce	7	you, him
3	too, from	8	again
4	who	9	This
5	do		

Exercise 4

▶ **1.4** Students work in pairs to match the questions with the responses. Then play the listening again to check.

Answers
2 d 3 h 4 f 5 a 6 e 7 g 8 b

Exercise 5

Students practise the conversation in pairs and then swap roles to do the same conversation again. You could ask the person giving Carmen's responses to cover the right-hand part of **4** so they can't see the answers when they respond.

Exercise 6

▶ **1.5** Write the two exchanges on the board and play the listening, pausing after each target sentence to elicit the main stressed words. Ask individual students to repeat the sentences with the same stress. You could point out that the expression *How / What about you?* is often enough to show that you are asking the same question again, so Carmen's questions *What do you do?* and *Why are you here?* aren't absolutely necessary.

Answers
1 What about <u>you</u>? What do <u>you</u> do?
2 How about <u>you</u>? Why are <u>you</u> here?

Carmen stresses these words because she is asking the same question that Gianluca asked her.

Further practice

If students need more practice, go to *Practice file 1* on page 106 of the *Student's Book*.

Exercise 7

Refer students to the example sentences and ask students which of the prompts the information corresponds to (*Name* and *Country*). Then elicit what questions they need to ask for the other prompts. If students are from the same company and/or country, you could ask them to invent a new identity for themselves. Then let them develop their conversation in pairs. Monitor their conversations and correct them if they aren't stressing the right words.

PRE-WORK LEARNERS   Ask students to invent a new identity for themselves. They could use different role cards from the teacher resources in the *Online practice* if necessary.

Exercise 8

Divide the students into groups of five or six. Elicit why conferences are important for business people (they are a good chance to make new contacts).

Students could use their own identity or the one they used for **7**. They could use different role cards if necessary.

Students stand up and walk around as if at an event. You could tell them they have to make three new friends/contacts. In addition, they have to introduce their new contacts to a third person if possible.

Give some feedback about their language performance. Correct one or two common errors, but not too many, and keep this mostly positive.

ONE-TO-ONE   You could take the roles of several different people at the conference, and suggest your student introduces him/herself to you. You could use different role cards from the teacher resources in the *Online practice* if necessary.

Photocopiable worksheet

Download and photocopy *Unit 1 Business communication worksheet* from the teacher resources in the *Online practice*.

Talking point

Refer students to the rules of the game, on page 136 of the *Student's Book*. They are fairly self-explanatory. Check students understand the rules. You could do a trial run of one or two 'goes' with the whole class.

▶ **1.6** Note that the questions for the 'Joker' squares are both on the listening and on page 144 of the *Student's Book*. However, since the pairs will be playing at different speeds, and reaching these squares at different moments, it will probably be easier for them to call you over and for you to read out the questions. An alternative would be to give the Joker questions (and the answers) to one member of each group to read out.

Answers to Joker questions
1 Google
2 Rolls-Royce
3 Sony
4 Boeing
5 Pirelli
6 Nokia
7 Danone

ONE-TO-ONE   To make sure the student gets the maximum practice in the language on the board, give them the chance to answer first each time. If they answer correctly on their turn, they proceed as per the normal rules. If they answer correctly on your turn, you must stay in the same place.

Progress test

Download and photocopy *Unit 1 Progress test* and *Speaking test* from the teacher resources in the *Online practice*.

2 Contacts

Unit content

By the end of this unit, students will be able to
- describe their job and the people they work with
- talk about work activities using the present continuous
- give phone numbers and spell names
- make and receive phone calls.

Context

The topic of this unit *Contacts* will be relevant to all business people. Making contact with people from within your company or from outside is an essential part of business life as an increasing number of tasks are outsourced, companies become more internationalized, and employees have an increasing amount of contact with customers and suppliers. Much of this interaction involves exchanging information and ideas, and giving support, and is carried out on the phone. Indeed, many jobs are conducted almost 100% over the phone or using video-conferencing equipment. However, doing business over the phone in a foreign language without the aid of non-verbal clues can lead to misunderstandings and, therefore, lost business. Your students will need effective ways of checking and clarifying information. Small talk, whether on the phone or face-to-face, is crucial for building good working relationships, and being able to introduce yourself or someone else and give basic information about a company is a basic requirement within this context.

In this unit, students learn how to talk about companies in general, as well as their own company, and their job in terms of what it involves, what roles there are and their current activities. The unit also deals with some set phrases needed in English to talk on the phone effectively, specifically checking information, as well as appropriate questions and responses when meeting and introducing people. Finally, students have the chance to compare their own workloads with those of people questioned in an international survey, carry out their own mini-survey, and imagine what parts of their job they would delegate to an assistant.

Starting point

Elicit ideas for 1 from the whole class, then ask them to discuss 2 in pairs.

PRE-WORK LEARNERS For question 1, ask students to think about their regular communication with people, and what ratio of it is on the phone as opposed to face-to-face. For question 2, ask students to consider how much time they spend speaking with fellow students, staff or professors, and how much studying alone.

> **EXTRA ACTIVITY**
> Before answering question 2, you could review some expressions of frequency. Write the words *time* and *a week* on the board and the following words randomly around them: *a little, a lot of, most of my, once, twice, three times, one day, three hours*. Students have to decide which of the expressions go with the word *time*, and which with the words *a week*.

Possible answers
a little / a lot of / most of my with *time*
once / twice / three times / one day / three hours with *a week*

Working with words

Exercise 1

Write the three jobs on the board. Check the pronunciation, particularly *psychologist*. Explain if necessary that *retail* is the sale of products directly to the public (so a shop is a *retailer*). Elicit some ideas from the whole class on what the three jobs consist of, but don't confirm the answers yet.

Exercise 2

Students read the text and compare their answers in pairs. Ask if their definitions in **1** were correct.

Answers
1 Retail buyer: a person who buys goods or services for a shop or chain of shops
2 Public relations officer: the person inside a company who works on the public image of the company, media relations, etc.
3 Business psychologist: a person who studies the working relationships of employees to make the company more effective and/or increase job satisfaction.

Exercise 3

Students read the text again and answer the questions.

Answers
1 Heidi (and Ben)
2 Sara, Ben
3 Sara
4 Heidi

Note that we use work *for* a company when we are actually employed by that company. We use work *with* a company when we have dealings with another company, or we are self-employed and work at their site for a limited period.

Exercise 4

Students work individually to match the words with their definitions, and then compare answers in pairs. Check answers with the whole class.

Answers
1 suppliers
2 employment agency
3 colleagues
4 clients
5 consultant
6 customers
7 staff

PRONUNCIATION Write the word *company* on the board with its three syllables marked (*com – pa – ny*). Explain that the first syllable has the stronger stress: com*pany*. Students then put the other words in the exercise into groups of the same stress pattern. Get them to say the words aloud and give them the correct pronunciation if necessary.

Answers
suppliers, consultant, employment
agency, customers
colleagues, training
staff

Exercise 5

Encourage students to develop their answers by saying *where*, *when* and *why* they work with the different people.

PRE-WORK LEARNERS Ask students to think of a job at a company that they have had, or would like, and to answer the question with this in mind.

Exercise 6

▶ **2.1** Before playing the listening, check students know what *software* is. You might also want to pre-teach *sales rep* (someone who sells the company's products or services).

Let students compare answers in pairs then check with the whole class.

Answers
1 sales rep
2 sales department
3 a team of two other reps, customers
4 time

Exercise 7

▶ **2.1** Ask students to try to guess or remember the missing words in pairs, then play the listening again and check the answers with the whole class.

Answers
1 produces
2 calculate, product
3 supplier
4 employs
5 organize, training

Exercise 8

Refer students to the *Tip*, then to the table. Ask them for examples of nouns in the same family as *sell* (*sales, sales rep,*

seller). Students complete the table alone, then compare answers in pairs. Check answers with the whole class.

Answers
produce (v), product
supplier
calculate (v)
employ (v), employee
organize (v)
training
consultant

Point out the different word stress on em*ploy*er and employ*ee*.

DICTIONARY SKILLS
Ask students to choose two words from **8** to check in a dictionary: what other related words can they find in other parts of speech (e.g. adjectives or nouns)? (e.g. *production; consulting* (firm), etc.

Further practice

If students need more practice, go to *Practice file 2* on page 108 of the *Student's Book*.

Exercise 9

Write *Where do you come _____?* on the board and ask students which word is missing. Point out that in questions with a preposition like *from, with, on* or *in*, the preposition is usually at the end. In many other languages, it's the first word of the question.

Students complete the questions and compare with a partner. To help them with the word *area* in question 2, give or ask them for example answers, e.g. *I work in sales, production, education,* etc.

Students can then ask you all the questions and you can answer either with details of your own job or another one you can invent. (If it's invented, can they guess which job it is?)

Answers
1 for
2 in
3 with
4 on
5 with

Exercise 10

While students are asking and answering the questions, monitor and make a note of both correct and incorrect uses of target vocabulary from this section. Write these examples on the board at the end and ask students to find the mistakes.

PRE-WORK LEARNERS Introduce a game element. Students answer the questions for a job of their choice and their partner has to guess which job it is. You could suggest a maximum of ten yes/no questions to guess each other's job. Demonstrate the activity yourself first.

Photocopiable worksheet

Download and photocopy *Unit 2 Working with words worksheet* from the teacher resources in the *Online practice*.

Language at work

Exercise 1

Students look at the pictures and answer the questions in pairs. Point out that for question 2, they should say what they *think* the people are talking about. Then get a few possible answers from the class. Accept all answers at this point, regardless of what tense they use.

> **Possible answers**
> 1 A: at a trade fair or conference; B: in the company car park, in front of the company; C: in the office
> 2 A: products they have seen or want to buy, the jobs they do; B: their work, what they're doing today or where they're going. Maybe one of the people is visiting the other's company; C: a document or report they're writing, a computer problem

Exercise 2

▶ **2.2** As an initial task, ask students to say what the people are talking about and compare their answers with question 2 from **1**. Then refer them to the three questions in this exercise and play the listening again, pausing where necessary to allow them time to note the responses. Ask the students for the responses and note them on the board. Ask them if each sentence is in the present continuous or present simple form.

> **Answers**
> 1 I'm a sales rep.
> 2 I'm travelling a lot more.
> 3 I'm just finishing this report.

Exercise 3

Students complete the explanations in the *Language point* individually, and then compare answers in pairs. Check the answers with the group. Point out that the term *around the present time* in explanation 2 could mean for example *today, this week, this month* or *this year*, depending on context.

> **Answers**
> 1 present continuous, I'm just finishing this report.
> 2 present continuous, I'm travelling a lot more.
> 3 present simple, I'm a sales rep.
> 4 *be*
> 5 *be, -ing* form of verb

> ┃ **Grammar reference**
> ┃ If students need more information, go to the *Grammar reference* on page 109 of the *Student's Book*.

Exercise 4

Check understanding by asking students to give one or two examples, then let them work in pairs. Monitor and ask students to self-correct if you hear any incorrect use of present simple or present continuous forms.

PRE-WORK LEARNERS Ask students to work in pairs, and to tell each other three things they do regularly at college and three things they are working on or studying at the moment.

Exercise 5

▶ **2.3** Tell students they are going to listen to two more conversations where people are using present simple and continuous forms. Let them listen and compare answers in pairs, then check answers with the whole class.

> **Answers**
> **Conversation 1**
> 1 access her files
> 2 NADI1374
> 3 a problem with the server
> **Conversation 2**
> 1 He's giving a training course.
> 2 a group of six people in telesales
> 3 Johann and the telesales team (but not Anabelle)

Exercise 6

▶ **2.3** Ask students to try and complete the conversation extracts in pairs. Then play Conversation 1 again, pausing to check the correct answers after each sentence.

> **Answers**
> 1 am, speaking
> 2 'm trying
> 3 isn't accepting
> 4 Is, working
> 5 is having

Exercise 7

▶ **2.3** Students work in pairs to make full sentences using the correct tenses. Explain that they don't have to reproduce the conversation word for word, just with the correct grammatical form. Then ask them for the correct questions and sentences and play Conversation 2 again to compare.

> **Answers**
> See audio script 2.3 on page 145 of the *Student's Book*.

Exercise 8

Students work in pairs and practise the conversation twice, swapping roles the second time around.

> ┃ **Further practice**
> ┃ If students need more practice, go to *Practice file 2* on page 109 of the *Student's Book*.

Exercise 9

Remind students of the situations in the two pictures, i.e. one conversation between people meeting for the first time, and another between people meeting each other again after a long time. Ask the class for questions that could be asked in each situation, then let them work in pairs. Monitor and make sure students are using the correct grammatical forms.

PRE-WORK LEARNERS Students could use an invented job, or a job they would like, or talk about their current course of study and their school or college. They could also use different role cards from the teacher resources in the *Online practice* if necessary.

> ┃ **Photocopiable worksheet**
> ┃ Download and photocopy *Unit 2 Language at work worksheet* from the teacher resources in the *Online practice*.

Practically speaking

Exercise 1
Refer students to the *Tip*, then ask them to answer the question. Elicit a range of answers.

Exercise 2
▶ **2.4** Students listen and write the numbers, and then compare answers with a partner. Check the answers together.

> **Answers**
> mobile: 0625 978033
> code for UK: 0044

Exercise 3
Students work in pairs, and exchange and note each other's phone numbers. Encourage them to check the numbers they've written down are correct, by saying *Can I repeat that back to you?*

Exercise 4
▶ **2.5** Students listen and then compare answers before you check with the whole class. Make a note of any confusion, e.g. between *a*, *e* and *i*, *g* and *j*, *p* and *b*, or *b* and *v*. Check pronunciation of letters as necessary.

> **Answers**
> 1 Geoff Eccleston
> 2 Aliny Reis

Note that in British English, *z* is pronounced 'zed', but in American English it is 'zee'.

Exercise 5
As in **3**, encourage students to check understanding by repeating the spelling of the names they've just noted. If they already know each other well or work/study in the same place, they could invent names and companies for themselves. Alternatively, they could also use different role cards from the teacher resources in the *Online practice* if necessary.

Business communication

Exercise 1
Ask students to answer the questions in pairs, then check the answers with the whole class. If the expressions they use aren't appropriate, ask them if they can improve on them, but don't provide any new language yet.

> **Possible answers**
> a I'm sorry, but I'm afraid he/she's not here / in a meeting / out of the office. Can I take / Would you like to leave a message?
> b No, thanks, I'm not interested. / I'm sorry, but / I'm afraid I don't have time. Can you call back later / another time?

Exercise 2
▶ **2.6** Students listen and match the conversations with the situations in **1**. Check answers with the whole class, then ask follow-up questions about the two conversations.
Conversation 1: *Who is the customer – the man or the woman?* (the woman) *Do you think the sales rep is happy with the call?*

Why/Why not? (No, because he didn't get the chance to tell her anything about the product.)
Conversation 2: *What's the reason for the call?* (to offer Leo some consultancy work) *What's the message?* (for Leo to call him back)

> **Answers**
> Conversation 1 b   Conversation 2 a

Exercise 3
▶ **2.6** Ask students to do the matching exercise individually and then compare answers in pairs. Then play Conversation 1 again. You can point out the following:
* We tend to say *This is ...* , not *I'm ...* to say who you are on the phone.
* We say *I'm calling ...* to give the reason for the call.
* The expression *Speaking* means *It's me speaking.*
* *You're welcome* is a standard response to somebody who thanks you.

> **Answers**
> 1 c   2 a   3 b   4 e   5 d

Exercise 4
Students decide who said which sentence/response. Go over the answers with the whole class.

> **Answers**
> Caller 1, 4, a, b, d
> Receiver 2, 3, 5, c, e

Exercise 5
Point out that the person receiving the call will answer with their own name and company name. Decide together who the caller would be (e.g. a university teacher for the first call and a sales rep for a training organization in the second) and invite students to choose a name for their university/organization. Then monitor their conversations and ask them to self-correct if you hear incorrect use of language.

Exercise 6
▶ **2.6** Students write the questions individually and then compare in pairs. Then play Conversation 2 again to check answers. Pause where necessary to allow time to note the responses.

> **Answers**
> Could I speak to Leo Keliher, please?
> Could I leave a message?
> Could I have your name, please?
> Could you ask Leo to call me back?
> Could you tell me what it's about?

Further practice
If students need more practice, go to *Practice file 2* on page 108 of the *Student's Book*.

Exercise 7
Ask students to read the two situations. Check they understand the instructions by asking *Who is the caller for the first/second conversation – A or B? What's the reason for the first/second call?* Then refer students to the *Key expressions* and give them time to prepare sentences they may need

for each call, either individually or in separate Student A and Student B groups. Then form A/B pairs and monitor their conversations for correct use of language, asking them to self-correct where necessary.

| Photocopiable worksheet
Download and photocopy *Unit 2 Business communication worksheet* from the teacher resources in the *Online practice*.

Talking point

As a lead-in, write *Modern working life* on the board with a happy emoticon to the left and an unhappy one to the right. Ask students to copy this down and then list in pairs the advantages and disadvantages under the relevant emoticon. Elicit one or two ideas first, if necessary, e.g. ☺ *more flexibility*; ☹ *longer hours*. Discuss their answers as a whole class.

Discussion

Exercise 1
Refer students to the infographic and ask them if any answers surprise them. Elicit a few comments from the class.

Exercise 2
Students discuss any similarities and differences with their own country. Share some of their answers to the group.

Exercise 3
Students consider what they would change in their own job to reduce the workload, and share answers in small groups.

Exercise 4
This exercise will work better in a larger class of ten or more students, where students can circulate and ask the questions to at least five other people and compile their own survey results. In a smaller group, you can ask the same questions to the whole class and list the results on the board. In both cases, encourage students not just to answer yes or no, but to give more details.

PRE-WORK LEARNERS Exercises 2 and 3 can be answered with reference to students' country and studies respectively.

ONE-TO-ONE Ask each other the survey questions. You could also suggest the student asks people he or she knows outside class who are currently working, and bring their answers back. The survey could be done in their own language if necessary, but the student should report back in English.

Task

Exercise 1
Refer students to the first sentence and get ideas briefly from the whole class of what sort of work they would give to an assistant. If necessary, point out that *Who* in the second question refers to the colleagues your assistant will need to work with, and that the question *What hours …?* means what times you want the assistant to be there (because maybe you are busier at certain times of the week).

Ask students if they would choose to delegate the tasks or activities they don't like themselves or give their assistant something more interesting. Then let them work alone on

their lists of regular and present activities. After five minutes, ask them for a few examples of each and check they are correctly using present simple and continuous forms.

PRE-WORK LEARNERS Ask students to imagine that the assistant will be there to help them with their studies.

Exercise 2
For this exercise, students discuss with their 'new assistant' their ideas from **1**. When they swap roles, and the new assistant becomes the 'boss' and vice versa, you can either keep the same pairs or change them around so that they talk and listen to somebody different. You may like to pre-teach the expressions *I need/want you to …* and *Do you need/want me to …?*; both are useful for talking about the assistant's responsibilities. At the end of the activity, ask the class who is offering the most interesting (or boring) assistant's job.

ONE-TO-ONE Use this opportunity to get as much information as possible about your student's job and make a note of the main responsibilities and the problems or challenges they face. This could be a useful source of information for future discussions or personalized role-plays.

| Progress test
Download and photocopy *Unit 2 Progress test* and *Speaking test* from the teacher resources in the *Online practice*.

Unit content

By the end of this unit, students will be able to

- describe a company's products and services
- talk about inventions
- show interest in a conversation
- give a research report.

Context

The topic of this unit *Products & services* is important in the business world. In a technological age, products and services are constantly being developed. While differentiating between products and services is less clear with so much available and accessible online, it's still a worthwhile distinction. In addition, as consumers, business people often like to keep up with and be aware of new developments and technologies. Many new products also have a role both in personal or social lives as well as business life; social media, for example, as well as online platforms and communication tools are key in business, as well as in liaising with friends and family.

In this unit, students have the opportunity to learn and talk about the benefits of products and services, and criteria for evaluating them, which is needed in talking about their own companies in the presence of clients as well as colleagues. They also learn to use the past simple to talk about the history of well-known products and the entrepreneurs who created them, as well as their own adoption of these products. They practise showing interest in what another speaker is saying, a reflex which is often lacking in students of this level because they don't know which expressions to use. They also have practice in giving a short oral presentation to summarize in a structured way the results of a market research study. Finally, they assess the value to them of four well-known technological products and nominate 'the greatest product of all time'.

Starting point

Students read the questions. You could elicit one or two examples, e.g. digital gadgets, food, drink and online services, to get them started. Allow time for them to consider their responses in pairs, then compare answers as a group.

Working with words

Exercise 1

Students work individually to consider if they agree or disagree with each sentence, and then discuss in pairs. You can then ask students to raise their hands to see which statements they agreed with most before asking for a few comments on why they made these choices.

Exercise 2

Explain that the text is about what most people want from products they buy and what their opinions are. Ask students to compare the five sentences in **1** with the five main points in the article: do most customers have the same opinion as the people in **1**? Students might need help with *advice* (uncountable), *efficiently, faulty, gadget*.

> **Answers**
> 1 Not true for most people – it's not just a question of low prices.
> 2 True
> 3 True – we want to know that companies can keep their promises.
> 4 Not true – there are some very good cheap products.
> 5 True

PRONUNCIATION Check sounds and stress in the following words: advice (n) /əd'vaɪs/; to advise (vb) /əd'vaɪz/; efficiently /ɪ'fɪʃntli/; gadget /'gædʒɪt/; reliable /rɪ'laɪəbl/; value /'væljuː/.

Exercise 3

Students look back at the survey again and discuss in pairs whether they agree with the order, and why/why not. Then elicit ideas from the whole class.

Exercise 4

Students complete the descriptions with words from **2**, and then compare answers in pairs before whole-class feedback. Then refer students to the *Tip* and ask them to find the example in **4** where the adjective goes before the noun (sentence 5). If students speak languages in which adjectives agree with the nouns they qualify, you can also point out that adjectives don't change their form in English, e.g. *Our staff are helpful* (no final 's'); *Our products are the best* (no final 's'). You could then ask them to transform other sentences in **4** to give a few other examples of adjectives before nouns, e.g. 1 *We provide a reliable service*.

Answers
1 reliable
2 user-friendly
3 good value
4 high-quality (or reliable)
5 popular
6 high-tech
7 original
8 helpful

Exercise 5

Elicit what types of products and services the pictures represent, then ask students to work in pairs. Get feedback from the whole class.

Possible answers
Bank: reliable, popular, helpful (staff), user-friendly (website)
Tablet computer: reliable, high-tech; high-quality
Online travel agency: reliable, user-friendly, good value, popular
Clothes shop: original, high-quality, helpful (staff), good value

Exercise 6

▶ **3.1** Students listen and match, and compare answers in pairs before you check with the group. They may need help with the following 'extreme' adjectives: *fantastic, amazing, great*.

Answers
1 Tablet computer: high-tech, high-definition, high-speed, super fast, popular, fantastic
2 Clothes shop: high-quality, original
3 Bank: safe, reliable, guaranteed, user-friendly, (easy)
4 Online travel agency: fantastic, great, amazing, good value, helpful

Exercise 7

▶ **3.1** Ask students to complete the sentences, then check answers with the group. Put three symbols: +++, ++ and + on the board and ask students to group the adverbs according to how 'strong' they are (*totally/really/extremely*, *very* and *pretty/quite* respectively). Check the answers together.

Answers
1 totally
2 really
3 quite
4 extremely
5 very
6 pretty

Exercise 8

Students use the sentences to talk about products and services they know. Elicit or give an example to start with, e.g. *I use the TripAdvisor website for checking restaurants. It's quite reliable, but not always*; or *The flight was extremely good value, and we didn't have to pay for extra suitcases.* After the pairwork, elicit a few examples from the whole class.

PRONUNCIATION Point out that using these adverbs and adjectives demonstrates the speaker's emotions, so it's important to use your voice to match this: we can do this by putting the stress on the adverb, i.e. <u>totally</u> new; <u>really</u> high quality. Students could listen again to listening 3.1 to hear which words are stressed.

Further practice
If students need more practice, go to *Practice file 3* on page 110 of the *Student's Book*.

Exercise 9

Working alone, students think of a company, shop or product, and compile a lists of words they could use to describe it.

Then ask them to read point 2: they will be recommending their company/shop/product to their partner, using the words. Give them time to prepare what they want to say. In turns, each student recommends the item to their partner. While they are doing this, listen out for accurate use of vocabulary.

When they have finished, invite specific recommendations from the whole class: students may enjoy sharing information about good shopping opportunities with the others! You could write any mistakes on the board afterwards, and ask the group to correct them.

Photocopiable worksheet
Download and photocopy *Unit 3 Working with words worksheet* from the teacher resources in the *Online practice*.

Language at work

Exercise 1

Students decide which inventions are the most important to them. Invite a couple of opinions before letting them discuss in pairs. Then try to establish a consensus with the class on the most important inventions.

Exercise 2

Ask students to try to match the inventions in **1** with their inventor and year, and then check in pairs. Don't provide the answers yet as they will be listening for these in **3**.

Exercise 3

▶ **3.2** Students listen to the radio programme to check their answers in **2**, and then compare answers in pairs. Go over the answers with the whole class and ask students if they were surprised by any of the answers.

Answers
Twitter: Jack Dorsey – 2006
Mobile phone: Martin Cooper – 1973
World Wide Web: Tim Berners-Lee – 1991
Smart cards: Roland Moreno – 1974

Exercise 4

Students match sentences 1–4 in the *Language point* to their explanations. Point out that the sentences are all from the listening in **3**. Ask students to do the matching exercise individually, then check with the whole class. Ask students to identify the irregular verbs in the four sentences and see if they know the past simple forms of *know* and *begin*.

Answers
1 a 2 c 3 d 4 b

Grammar reference
If students need more information, go to *Grammar reference* on page 111 of the *Student's Book*.

Exercise 5

▶ **3.3** Students listen to the story of Jack Dorsey and Twitter, and order the events. On the second listening, pause the listening each time one of the events is mentioned to allow students to note their answers. Students compare answers in pairs after each listening before checking with you.

Answers
9   People don't understand why Twitter is necessary
7   Starts a new company with two other people
3   Goes to New York University
4   Doesn't finish his studies
10 Presidential candidates use Twitter
2   Studies in Missouri
6   Sells software online
5   Moves to California
1   Produces software for taxi drivers
8   Creates a website in two weeks

DICTIONARY SKILLS
Ask students to work in pairs to decide which verbs in **5** are regular and irregular and what the past simple forms are. They can then check these by looking up the verbs in the dictionary. You may need to point out how the verb forms are indicated in the dictionary entry.

Exercise 6

Refer students to the *Tip*. Practise the pronunciation of the four verbs, then ask them to identify the regular verbs in **5** and put them in two categories: extra syllable (*started*, *created*) and no extra syllable (*finished*, *used*, *studied*, *moved*, *produced*). Ask them to practise saying these, too. They then take turns with a partner to tell the story of Jack Dorsey. Monitor the pairwork, asking students to self-correct if they make a mistake in past simple forms.

Suggested answer
He produced software for taxi drivers. He studied in Missouri. He went to New York University, but he didn't finish his studies. He moved to California where he sold software online. He started a new company with two other people and created a website in two weeks. At first, people didn't understand why Twitter was necessary, but in 2008 the two Presidential candidates used Twitter.

Further practice
If students need more practice, go to *Practice file 3* on page 111 of the *Student's Book*.

Exercise 7

Elicit from students what they learnt about Roland Moreno and Martin Cooper in **3**, and let them decide in their pairs who will read about each inventor. They then read the relevant pages and make notes. Check they understand *smart card technology* (student A), and *device* and *portable* (student B). Ensure they write short notes and not complete sentences.

Answers

	Roland Moreno	**Martin Cooper**
Main invention	Smart card	Mobile phone (Dyna-TAC)
School/ Education	Paris – didn't finish his studies	Illinois Institute of Technology – Masters (1957)
Job(s)	Worked for newspapers then created own company Innovatron	Motorola
Launch date of invention	25th March 1974	3rd April 1973
First success	1983 – France Télécom used technology for phone card	1983 – first commercial mobile phone service
Other inventions	Musical instruments, including the 'pianok' portable piano	1967 – first portable police radio system

Exercise 8

Elicit the correct question forms from the whole class, then ask them to ask and answer the questions in pairs. Monitor the pairwork for correct past simple forms and ask students to self-correct where necessary. When they have finished, ask the whole class what they found interesting or surprising.

Answers
What did he invent?
Where did he go to school?
Who did he work for?
When did he launch his invention?
When did his invention become a success?
Did he invent any other products?

Exercise 9

Students discuss their experiences of products and services in **1** using the questions. Monitor their discussions, and write on the board three correct and two incorrect past simple sentences you hear. When students have finished, ask them to find the incorrect sentences and to correct them.

Photocopiable worksheet
Download and photocopy *Unit 3 Language at work worksheet* from the teacher resources in the *Online practice*.

Practically speaking

Exercise 1

▶ **3.4** You could start by modelling how strange it looks or sounds when you don't show interest, e.g. by asking a student to tell you about what he/she did last weekend and asking the other students to watch and listen to you. Then just look at the student while he's/she's speaking without commenting or responding in any way. Ask the class to say what was wrong.

Then refer students to the exercise. After listening, check answers with the whole class.

Exercise 2

▶ **3.4** Students may be able to complete the extracts
without listening again. If so, you can refer them directly to
the *Tip*. Play the listening again, and say on which words (or
on which part of the word) the voice of the speaker changes,
and if the voice goes up or down. Ask them to repeat
what they hear and provide a model yourself if necessary.
Demonstrate by saying the phrases more slowly. Encourage
them to repeat the sentences after you.

Exercise 3

Students practise the exchanges in pairs. Monitor their
pronunciation carefully and make sure their intonation
makes them sound interested.

Exercise 4

Students follow the instructions and try to keep their
conversations going as long as possible.

Business communication

Exercise 1

Students work in pairs to look at the picture and discuss the
questions. Elicit feedback briefly from the whole class.

Exercise 2

▶ **3.5** Students listen to the research report on the use of
podpads. There is a lot of information to note, so you might
like to ask them not to write anything the first time they
listen. Play the listening once without stopping and allow
students time to compare answers in pairs. Then play the
listening a second time, pausing when each question has
been answered by the presenter to allow students time to
write. Let them compare answers in pairs before checking
together.

Check students understand *to install*.

ALTERNATIVE As there is a lot of information to listen to, you
could suggest students work in pairs: Student A notes down
answers to the first and third questions, and Student B notes
down answers to the second and fourth question. Students
then discuss their shared answers together.

Exercise 3

▶ **3.5** Students work in pairs to match 1–10 to a–j to make
sentences. Then play the listening again for students to
check. Students might ask the difference between *to find out*
in sentence 2 and *(we) found* in sentence 6. Point out that we
normally *find out* something by asking questions or receiving
information. *(We) found* means we learnt or discovered.

Remind students that *research* (n) is uncountable, e.g. *some /
a piece of research*.

Further practice

If students need more practice, go to *Practice file 3* on page
110 of the *Student's Book*.

Exercise 4

Students read the questions, and then work in pairs to ask
and answer them. Elicit a few answers to the first question
to get them started. After four or five minutes, elicit some of
their findings from the group.

Exercise 5

As a lead-in, ask students why a company might want its
employees to have a short sleep after lunch (to work better
in the afternoon). Does the idea exist in their country? Would
they like to have this possibility in their company? Then refer
them to the two pictures – which type of bed would they
prefer? Why?

Divide the class into As and Bs. Each looks at their relevant
page. Check they understand *volunteer*. Allow time for
students to read their information and prepare their reports,
individually or in pairs. Refer them also to the *Key expressions*.

Point out that the verbs in the information they have are in the present, but they will need to change some to the past simple to report on what they did.

Then form A+B pairs. Each pair gives a report in turn, and together they decide which of the beds is better. Encourage use of the language from **3** and **4** and *Key expressions*. Listen in and note down any language you want to highlight.

When they have finished, elicit answers from the whole group; you could have a class vote on the best bed!

Check the use of report language from **3**. Point out examples of good use of language and any common mistakes, especially in the target language.

ONE-TO-ONE Either give a report yourself on one of the ideas, after which the student gives theirs, or ask the student to give two reports.

Photocopiable worksheet
Download and photocopy *Unit 3 Business communication worksheet* from the teacher resources in the *Online practice*.

Talking point

As a lead-in, ask students to discuss in pairs what their favourite products are and why. You could demonstrate this first yourself. Get feedback on their ideas from the group.

> **EXTRA ACTIVITY**
> Tell students that the average family of four has eight screens in their house. Elicit what types of screen this could include (TV, computer, tablet, laptop, mobile phone, camera, satnav or GPS). Ask them to count how many screens they have in their home and see who has the most. Then ask them to consider these questions in pairs: *Do we need all those screens? Imagine a situation where you can only have three screens in your house. Which screens would you choose and why?*

Discussion

Exercise 1
▶ **3.6** Refer students to the four pictures. Ask them to name the products and say what they're used for. Ask them to read the two questions, and then play the listening (twice if necessary). Allow them to compare answers in pairs after each listening. Then check answers with the group and invite comments on whether they agree with the speakers.

Answers
Product 1 – an e-reader. Bought to make travelling easier, and not to have to take lots of books on holiday. Advantage(s): easy to transport; includes hundreds of books.
Product 2 – a SatNav. Bought because the person was not good at map-reading. Advantage(s): all the information is there; it's reliable; it finds another solution if you take the wrong route; it tells you when you will arrive.
Product 3 – a microwave. Bought because she forgot to drink her drinks while they were hot. Advantage(s): everyone in the family can use it; it's safer for young children than using a gas cooker.
Product 4 – a watch. Bought because it's user-friendly and simple.

Exercise 2
Students discuss in pairs if they use the products pictured, and why.

Exercise 3
Encourage students to give reasons for their answers, and then discuss one or two of their comments with the whole group.

Exercise 4
Encourage students to give reasons for their answers, and then discuss some of their ideas with the whole group, with reasons why. Find out which items are most popular, i.e. which ones they can't live without, and which ones are not important to them.

Task

Exercise 1
Students read the instructions. Discuss and agree on what you all understand by 'modern-day' and 'traditional', e.g. technological and non-technological products, or products made before or after the digital revolution. Elicit a few examples of products they might put in each category. Point out different types of products, e.g. for the home, for work, for health, education, travel, or sport.

Exercise 2
Students finalize their lists of traditional and modern-day products to three items in each group. When agreeing on their shortlists of products, encourage them to justify to each other why they have nominated these.

Exercise 3
Students think about ways to evaluate the products, e.g. good value; created a need that didn't exist before; makes life easier/safer/quicker/etc.; solved a problem that had no solution before; popular with many different ages, etc.

Exercise 4
Students use the criteria to decide which is the best product in each category.

Monitor and ask students to self-correct if you hear any mistakes in either present or past simple tenses as taught in the first three units of the book.

Finally, ask a person from each group to tell the class which product they chose in each category and why.

Progress test
Download and photocopy *Unit 3 Progress test* and *Speaking test* from the teacher resources in the *Online practice*.

Viewpoint 1

Exercise 1

▶ 01 Allow the students time to look at the question words, and to think about what questions they could make. Students then watch and decide what questions each person was asked. You could play the video more than once so that students can take notes, or elicit what the speakers say; this will help them work out the questions.

Exercise 2

▶ 02 Students watch the complete video and compare their questions in **1** with the questions used in the video. If necessary, pause after each question to allow writing time.

Answers
Who do you work for?
Which department do you work in?
What does your company specialize in?
Where is your company based?
How old is your company?
How many people does it employ?

Exercise 3

Ask the students to work in pairs and interview each other using the questions from the video. Try to put students with someone from a different company; alternatively, they could pretend they work for another company.

You could suggest they make videos of their interviews, and post them on a classroom blog so that they can watch the interview with all the students in class.

PRE-WORK LEARNERS Ask students to imagine they work for a company they know something about; they could make a few notes first, before interviewing each other. Alternatively, they could use the questions below:
Where are you studying?
What are you specializing in?
Where is your college?
When does your course finish?
How many people are there on your course?
What do you hope to do after the course?

Exercise 4

▶ 03 Give time for students to read the information in the box before playing the video. Then play Video 3, which is only pictures and has no script. They answer the questions individually. Don't check answers for now.

Exercise 5

Students work in pairs to discuss their answers, and give reasons.

Exercise 6

▶ 04 Students now watch the full video with Till Hahn, company director of Glasbau Hahn, to check their answers in **4**, and to add information about the company to the table.

Suggested answers

makes a product or provides a service	They make a product – windows, door fronts, glass doors, louvered windows, display cases, museum equipment.
is a modern or traditional company	Traditional, but also uses modern technology
employs lots of people	Quite big. They have 120 employees in Frankfurt, 35 in Stockstadt, and 15 in offices in Japan, China, the US and England.
works with international clients	Yes
is specialized and technical	Very specialized and technical

VIDEO SCRIPT

(Voiceover: Glasbau Hahn is a glass-making factory in Frankfurt in Germany. Till Hahn is its Director.)

Our company has been based from the very start always in Frankfurt am Main. Originally, we had been more in the centre of the city, but during World War II Frankfurt was heavily bombed, then we moved out a bit towards the East and this is where we are and where we feel very happy.
We can trace our company back to 1836, that's when my great-grandfather came to Frankfurt as a glazier and he married a widow who had been in the glass business already before, and ever since, it's in the hands of the Hahns.
Our company can be divided in three sections. The original one was strictly the glass business – windows, door fronts, glass doors, and so on. The second one is louvre windows – a special window for ventilation. Perhaps the most glamorous part of our business is display cases, museum equipment.

Who are your clients?
Well, when I talk about display cases, our clients certainly are museums – museums all around the world. After England we were brave enough to expand into the United States, that was my special effort for the company, which has turned out very well. And now we are doing business with most places on earth. We have, I think, six offices for representing us spread around.

How many employees do you have?
In Frankfurt we have about 120 employees, there are about another 35 in Stockstadt who are doing the louvre window business, and then we have about another 15 people in our various offices in Japan, in Tokyo, in China, in the United States and in England.

Who are your competitors?

There had been some glorious times in the past when we didn't have any competition, that was in 1935 when my father invented the first all glass construction, meaning the bonding of glass to glass without intermediate framing.

Then it was back in 1970 where competitors became more apparent and they are not so much in Germany, but rather one of the competitors is based in Italy, one is in England, and we always meet when there's an international bidding to do. And usually we are the most expensive one, but fortunately our clients nevertheless rank quality highest, and the price tag is not the only decision factor, otherwise it would be very … to our disadvantage. Our markets where we are very successful outside of England and America is lately, specially is Japan, very important, China, and even Egypt.

Exercise 7

▶ 04 Before playing the interview again, ask students to read the sentences, and guess what sort of information is missing. Then play the interview again, while students complete and check the sentences.

Check any difficult vocabulary, e.g. *trace* (vb): to find the origin of something; *louvre windows* (n): windows with angled, horizontal slats of glass; *bond* (vb): join firmly; *price tag* (n): a label on something that shows how much you must pay (sometimes figurative).

> **Answers**
> 1 Frankfurt am Main
> 2 1836
> 3 three, glass
> 4 clients
> 5 six
> 6 120, 35, 15
> 7 competition, England
> 8 China, Egypt

Exercise 8

Students work in pairs to compare their own company with Glasbau Hahn. Depending on who you have in your class, students could work first in same-company groups, and then re-pair with someone from another company to share their findings.

Elicit a few key findings from the class.

PRE-WORK LEARNERS Ask students to think of a local company, or one they know well, and compare it with Glasbau Hahn. They could check information and statistics about the company of their choice online first.

Exercise 9

Ask students to work with a different partner, read the sentences and consider the price, quality or other deciding factors in their service or product's success.

For feedback, ask each pair to give one key piece of information to the group.

PRE-WORK LEARNERS Students could think about a product or service they know well and compare it with a similar product made by a different manufacturer. Again, they could find some of the information online first. Alternatively, you could ask each student to research one product at home, in their own time; you could decide on or allocate these products or services in class so that everyone knows what the other is researching, e.g. different options for language

training in their city, fast food or quality restaurants, sports equipment and so on.

Further video ideas

You can find a list of suggested ideas for how to use video in the class in the teacher resources in the *Online practice*.

4 Visitors

Context

Visitors are a key element in business life. The visitor may be a potential investor or partner, or a new or regular supplier or client. In these days of globalization and multinational companies, the visitor may work for the same company or a subsidiary. Although companies are increasingly making use of conference-call and video-conferencing possibilities, it is still recognized that there is a need to visit a company's facilities and have direct face-to-face contact with the people concerned, especially in the early stages of a relationship.

As part of a visit, someone may be taken around a company to visit the different departments. It is important for the visitor to be able to ask questions about these departments and the people who work in them, and for the host to be able to answer them. Moreover, for the host, making your visitor feel welcome will certainly contribute to the success of their visit.

In this unit, students will learn to talk about the departments in a company and what people in those departments do, as well as describing the activity of their own department. Students will also have plenty of question practice both in asking about company structure and making visitors feel welcome. In the *Talking point*, they will have the chance to role-play a series of typical scenes from a company visit.

Starting point

Answer the first question with the whole class and help with the names of departments if necessary, but don't write anything on the board. Then let them discuss the second question in pairs before getting feedback on answers with the whole class.

PRE-WORK LEARNERS Make the first question hypothetical: *Which department would you like to work in?*

Working with words

Exercise 1

Ask students to do this in pairs. Note that they may already have the names of a few departments from the *Starting point*. If they don't know the names in English, encourage them to ask you questions beginning *What do you call the department where …?* Write the list from the class on the board.

> **Possible answers**
> The ten departments that feature in **5** + Training, After-sales, Engineering, Dispatch, Inventory, R + D, Costing

PRONUNCIATION You could write the names of each department on the board, ask students to identify the correct stress on each word, and mark it on the board.

Exercise 2

Ask students to work in pairs and divide the departments from your list into two categories – more important and less important – and to explain their choice by talking about their company. Be ready to stop this activity if students quickly reach the conclusion in the text that follows, i.e. that all departments are equally important in their company.

PRE-WORK LEARNERS As students don't have a department or company to speak about, ask them to talk about their general opinion of which departments are more or less important.

Exercise 3

Ask students to read and answer the questions individually, then quickly check the answers with the whole class.

> **Answers**
> Sales, Marketing, Finance, Purchasing, Accounts, Production, Quality Control, Logistics, Customer Service, Human Resources (HR), IT
> The writer says that all departments are equally important.

Exercise 4

After the pairwork, get feedback on answers with the whole class. Note that this exercise may be redundant if they have decided in **2** that all departments are equally important. If so, ask students if there is any competition between departments in their company, and whether it's positive or negative.

Exercise 5

Students complete the exercise individually, then check with a partner before whole-class feedback. Note that students may need help to pinpoint the meaning of the target verbs. These near synonyms may be useful: *dispatch* (send), *maintain* (keep in good condition), *generate* (create), *resolve* (find solutions to), *invoice* (send request for payment), *control* (manage), *recruit* (find).

Answers

1	dispatches	6	checks
2	maintains	7	manufactures
3	buys	8	invoices
4	generates	9	controls
5	resolves	10	recruits

PRONUNCIATION Focus on the different pronunciations of the third person 's': Say the ten verbs from **5** and ask students to listen for the ending and put them in the correct category. Then ask them to practise saying the sentences aloud in pairs.

Answers
/z/ maintains, buys, resolves, manufactures, controls
/s/ generates, checks, recruits
/ɪz/ dispatches, invoices

EXTRA ACTIVITY

Students work in threes. In turn, each student thinks of a department and mimes (or draws, without using any words) what the people work there do. The others have to guess. See which group can guess the most departments within a time limit of, e.g. five minutes.

Exercise 6

Ask students to draw or use an actual organization chart from their company. If they do not know, ask them to draw a diagram of the departments they work with.

PRE-WORK LEARNERS Ask students to research the organization chart of a company of their choice on the Internet, and then to present it.

Further practice

If students need more practice, go to *Practice file 4* on page 112 of the *Student's Book*.

Exercise 7

▶ 4.1 This activity allows students to listen for some of the department names from this unit, and introduces some expressions for describing company structure. Play the listening once or twice as necessary. Students compare answers in pairs before checking over answers with you.

Answers

Person	A	B	C
Works in	Finance	Logistics	HR
Usually works with	Accounts	Production and Sales	all departments
Meeting today with	IT	Purchasing	Director of HR

Exercise 8

▶ 4.1 Students listen again and complete the sentences.

Answers
1 work, with
2 responsible for
3 charge of
4 contact with
5 report to

Exercise 9

Monitor and ask students to self-correct if you hear any incorrect use of the target language.

PRE-WORK LEARNERS Students decide which department they 'work' for but don't tell their partner. When answering the questions, they shouldn't mention the name of the department at all, and their partner has to guess. (Suggest students don't ask and answer questions 3 and 4.)

Photocopiable worksheet

Download and photocopy *Unit 4 Working with words worksheet* from the teacher resources in the *Online practice*.

Language at work

Exercise 1

You could start by asking students to imagine they are visiting another company for the first time. What kind of questions could they ask? You could give students a sheet of A4 and ask them to write, in large letters, their ideas for questions; you can then stick them on the board. Don't offer any correction for the moment, but tell students you will look at their questions again in a few minutes.

Then refer students to the exercise. They complete the questions individually, then check with a partner before asking and answering the questions in pairs. Monitor the pairwork and ask students to self-correct if you hear any mistakes in tense use in the answers.

Answers
1 When   2 How many   3 Which   4 Who   5 How often
6 Did   7 Is

Exercise 2

Students answer the questions in pairs before you check with the whole class. They may need reminding of the difference between an auxiliary and a main verb, and they may have particular difficulty with the *Why?* questions in 4 and 5.

Refer students to the *Tip* about *which* and *what*. Ask them why the first four questions in the *Language point* begin with the word *Which?* rather than *What?* To check their understanding, elicit some other examples of questions using the two different question words.

Answers
1 Questions 1, 3 and 5
2 The auxiliary verb
3 Questions 6 and 7
4 Question 7. There is no auxiliary verb when *be* is the main verb.
5 Because the question word or phrase is the subject of the question.

Grammar reference

If students need more information, go to *Grammar reference* on page 113 of the *Student's Book*.

Exercise 3

Ask students to complete the questions individually before checking answers with the group. Then refer them to the questions on the board from **1** and ask them to say if they are correct or not. If there are mistakes, ask them to correct them.

Students then ask and answer the questions from this exercise with a partner.

Answers
1 Do
2 leaves
3 do you
4 Is
5 work

PRE-WORK LEARNERS When students have completed the questions with the correct option, ask each student to invent a job for themselves and to decide on their answers to each question. Then put them in pairs to ask and answer the questions.

Exercise 4

▶ **4.2** You may like to start by reviewing company departments. Ask each student for the name of a department. Students then listen and compare answers in pairs. Ask them what key words in each extract helped them to find the departments. Check answers with the whole class.

Answers
Extract 1 Finance
Extract 2 HR
Extract 3 Customer service
Extract 4 Sales

Exercise 5

▶ **4.2** Students do this individually, then compare answers with a partner. Listen to check, pausing after each question.

Answers
1 How often does he work in this office? (about one day a week)
2 Where does he come from? (New York, America)
3 How long are you staying here? (two days)
4 How many people work in Human Resources? (six)
5 When did you open this building? (two months ago)
6 Are all the staff fluent in English? (no)
7 Who chooses your sales markets? (markets and sales director)
8 Which countries are interested in your products? (Sweden and Denmark, some interest from Poland)
9 Do you know the Polish market well? (no)

PRONUNCIATION Usually, intonation on questions with a question word will go down. Yes/No questions usually end with the intonation going up. Suggest students listen again to the questions in **5**, pausing after each question for students to repeat.

Further practice

If students need more practice, go to *Practice file 4* on page 113 of the *Student's Book*.

Exercise 6

Let students prepare the questions in pairs, then check answers with the whole class.

Suggested answers
2 What time do I start and finish?
3 Where/When do I have lunch? / How long do we get for lunch?
4 Do we have coffee or tea breaks?
5 Where's the photocopier? / How do I use it?
6 Do I need a key or security pass?
7 Where is the restroom?
8 Is there a car park? / Can I use the car park? / Where can I park my car?
9 When do we receive our salaries?
10 Who is the administrator?

EXTENSION Ask stronger students, or early finishers, to think of three more things they would ask questions about, e.g. a password to use the photocopier; a café or restaurant nearby, etc.

Exercise 7

Students ask and answer all the questions playing the same roles. They then swap roles and do the same again. Monitor and be ready to provide help with vocabulary as necessary because the open nature of the activity may mean students need new terms they haven't learnt yet.

PRE-WORK LEARNERS Students invent the information, so they may need a little time to prepare their answers before doing the role-play. You could ask one student from each pair to imagine a department where rules are very strict, and the other student one which is more relaxed.

Photocopiable worksheet

Download and photocopy *Unit 4 Language at work worksheet* from the teacher resources in the *Online practice*.

Practically speaking

Exercise 1

Students read the instructions and then think of the words they can use to complete the questions. Elicit possible answers from the whole class. They will probably give the answer *Does* for question 1, and may try to produce a question tag for 2 or 3 or have no idea. Don't provide the answers for the moment.

Exercise 2

▶ **4.3** Listen and elicit the answers from the whole class. Elicit or point out if necessary why we say *Doesn't* and not *Does* in question 1 (it shows that we think we are right but want to confirm the information).

Point out also that when we use a question tag as in question 3, we use the same auxiliary verb as in the question form but in the negative, e.g. *He went to the trade fair* (past simple) = **Did** *he go to the trade fair?* (question) = *He* **went** *to the trade fair,* **did***n't he?* (question tag). To check their understanding, ask them what the question tag would be for question 2 (*doesn't he*).

Note that this may be the first time students have seen question tags and they will probably find them difficult to form. You can point out that if they are in any doubt when speaking, they can usually just tag the word … *right?* to the end of their question, as in question 2.

Answers
1 Doesn't
2 right
3 didn't he

PRONUNCIATION On question tags, our voice goes down if we want to confirm that the information is true. However, if we're not sure, and it's actually a real question, the intonation usually goes up at the end. However, these speech patterns vary from culture to culture and person to person. For this unit section, the only important thing is that students do one or the other (rather than use flat intonation) to indicate that this is a question.

Exercise 3

Do this with the whole class first, as you will probably need to provide help with question structures. Note that in questions 2, 3 and 5 we use the auxiliary *be* rather than *do*, but you can point out that the question tag follows the same rule as indicated in **2**, e.g. *She's in charge – **Is** she in charge? – She's in charge, **is**n't she?*

Then let students practise the different forms in pairs, and monitor for correct forms and intonation. For stronger students, help them with the intonation, reminding them if they are only asking for confirmation, the intonation goes down, but that if it's a real question, the intonation goes up.

Answers
You can add … *right?* To all sentences to make questions or
2 Isn't she in charge of Accounts? She's in charge of Accounts, isn't she?
3 Isn't he coming to the meeting? He's coming to the meeting, isn't he?
4 Doesn't she live in London? She lives in London, doesn't she?
5 Aren't you from Hamburg? You're from Hamburg, aren't you?
6 Didn't I meet you yesterday? I met you yesterday, didn't I?

Exercise 4

Students need time to think of the five pieces of information before asking the questions. You may need to give them ideas for this, e.g. present job, last job, home town, family, likes/dislikes, last weekend, etc. If students don't know each other well enough, you could ask each person to write down five pieces of information, three of which are true and two not exactly true. They then give the list to their partner, who then asks the confirming question.

Business communication

Exercise 1

Students read the question. Elicit possible questions from the whole class and give feedback on whether their questions are good, could be better or are not appropriate – but don't suggest alternatives for the moment. You may like to note the good questions on a prominent part of the board and those that need improving on a piece of paper to deal with later.

Possible answers
The following are all possible:
Did you have a good trip or journey? Did you find the company without any problems? Is your hotel OK? Would you like a coffee/something to drink? Is this your first visit? Do you know our town/this area? How long are you here for/are you staying? Do/Will you have time to visit the town/area? What would you like to do during your stay?
Students may also find other useful questions within this section they can use.

PRE-WORK LEARNERS Ask students to imagine they work for a company, and have a visitor from abroad (e.g. a client, or partner) coming in today. What questions could they ask, e.g. about their journey, where they are staying, etc. Give them three minutes in pairs to think of some questions.

Exercise 2

▶ 4.4 Listen to all three conversations without stopping, and let students compare their answers in pairs. Then listen again if necessary, stopping after each conversation to give them time to compare again. Check answers with the whole class at the end.

Answers
1 She asks him to show some identification and to sign in. She gives him a visitor's pass.
2 His flight arrived on time, but he was a little late because of the bad traffic. Olivia takes him to her office.
3 He asks for a coffee, a socket to plug in his computer and an Internet connection. He wants to check his email first.

Exercise 3

Let students do this in pairs but be ready to offer extra help, as students will probably only remember or be able to guess some of the missing words. If you feel it's necessary, write all the missing phrases randomly around the board and ask students to match them to the gaps in sentences 1–10. Don't check answers with the whole class for the moment. Note that the host is the person receiving the visitor.

Alternatively, you could listen to the conversations again, but don't do this if they have taken a long time to find the answers to **2**.

Exercise 4

Students do this individually and then compare answers with a partner. They may need help with the meaning of the expression *No hurry*. The phrases *Here you are* and *After you* can be explained with a simple mime if necessary.

Exercise 5

▶ 4.4 Stop the listening after each sentence and response and elicit the answers to **3** and **4**. For the oral practice, one student in each pair plays the role of the visitor, and the other the receptionist, then the host. They then switch roles. You could then ask them to cover the responses and do it again so they are giving the responses from memory.

If you noted down any questions that needed improving or were inappropriate in **1**, ask students to correct them now based on what they've learnt in this section.

Further practice

If students need more practice, go to *Practice file 4* on page 112 of the *Student's Book*.

Exercise 6

If you think students need time to plan their conversation carefully, put them in AA and BB pairs first, with As preparing the visitor's role, and Bs preparing the receptionist's/host's role; monitor and help students with question and answer ideas where necessary. You could also suggest they take notes. Once they have role-played one conversation, they could repeat it, swapping roles. Monitor the conversations for correct use of expressions and appropriately enthusiastic (not flat) intonation.

Possible answers

In reception

Visitor: I have an appointment with … Thank you for inviting me.
Receptionist: Can you sign in, please? Can I see some identification? Please take a seat. He'll/She'll be right there.
Host: Nice to meet you / see you again. Thank you for coming. Did you have a good trip / any trouble finding us? Let's go to the meeting room. It's this way.

On the way to meeting room

Visitor: How many people work here? Which department do you work in? When did you start working here? How often do you have visitors? Who is here for the meeting today? Where's your office?, etc.

In meeting room

Host: This is / Here's the meeting room. Can I get you a coffee / anything else? Do you need an Internet connection / a video projector? Help yourself. There's a socket just there.
Visitor: Can I have some photocopies? I just need to make a quick phone call.

Photocopiable worksheet

Download and photocopy *Unit 4 Business communication worksheet* from the teacher resources in the *Online practice*.

Talking point

This game takes the 'players' through a typical visit to a company, starting with the initial welcome, then a tour of the company, getting ready for a meeting/presentation, and finally chatting socially over lunch or dinner.

Work through the rules of the game with the students. Emphasize that the aim is to ask more questions than their partner, but that their questions must be natural for the situation described. With weaker students, you might like to start by asking them to work in pairs on a list of questions that could be asked either by the visitor or the host using the question words given.

You may choose to impose the rule that only grammatically correct or appropriate sentences win a point. (Students will have to agree between them if a question is correct or not, and check with you if necessary.)

ALTERNATIVE Instead of swapping roles when students get to each new 'place', you could ask them to stay in role in the interests of continuity but set a time limit of, say, ten minutes after which the roles swap even if they haven't covered all the situations.

Possible answers

Questions could include the following (for visitor or host): **Is** this your first time here/the right entrance? **Are** you Mr. X? **Aren't** you the Marketing Director? **Do** you work here every day? **Don't** you have another office in London? **Does** the meeting room have a projector? **Doesn't** your boss work here too? **Did** you have a good trip? **Didn't** I see you in Paris last week? **Can I** get you / have a glass of water? **Can you** tell Mr Y I'm here? **Where**'s your office? **What** do you do exactly? **Which** department do you work in? **Who** do you want to see this afternoon? **Why** did you decide to work here? **When** did you move to these offices? **How** do you come to work? **How many** people live in this town?

Progress test

Download and photocopy *Unit 4 Progress test* and *Speaking test* from the teacher resources in the *Online practice*.

Unit content

By the end of this unit, students will be able to

- talk about customer service
- make comparisons
- soften a message when complaining
- make and deal with complaints.

Context

Customer service is a field which has become of increasing importance over recent years, as companies try to find the added value that will attract and, as importantly, retain customers. This field has even become a separate area of business expertise, with various 'gurus' being hired by companies to improve their performance.

A challenge that many businesses are facing is that of developing online sales while continuing to improve their customer service. The Internet offers quick solutions for customers and retailers to find each other, but it is important to ensure that this potentially more impersonal contact isn't at the expense of customer satisfaction or loyalty.

Another vital aspect of customer service is that of dealing with complaints. No company can avoid things occasionally going wrong, but the way in which it copes with that situation can make a strong positive impression on the customer – or a negative one. In this way, complaints can become an opportunity to improve customer relationships.

This unit focuses on customer service from two points of view: as workers (or potential workers) in companies that deal with customers, and as customers themselves. Students will learn the vocabulary necessary to talk about customer service practices and experiences. By contrasting these different practices, they will also learn how to make comparisons. They will then practise some useful expressions for making and dealing with customer complaints. In the *Talking point*, they will discuss with reference to specific customer experiences what constitutes exceptional customer service.

Starting point

You could start by asking students to think about bad experiences of customer service and what kind of things they find annoying. They can then discuss the questions as a whole class or initially in pairs. For question 2, you could ask them as a follow-up to formulate 'rules' for good customer service, starting with *Always …* and *Never …*

Working with words

Exercise 1

Students read and discuss the questions, as a whole class or in pairs.

Exercise 2

Students read individually and discuss the answers to the questions in pairs before whole-class feedback.

Possible answers

1 Customers have a wide choice of communication channels. Companies can learn more about their customers.
2 They can waste a lot of time explaining and re-explaining their problem to different people in the company.
3 They lose customers.

Exercise 3

Answer the question as a whole class. Encourage students to think about their own experience as consumers or employees in their own companies.

Possible answers

Thinking about <u>where</u> and <u>when</u> communication takes place, and whether other times or channels of communication are better, e.g. face-to-face vs. telephone or written communication; email, etc. Does the company website have a 'Contact us' option? What other forums for communication are available? You could ask students to think about which means are best for which sorts of customer issues.

Exercise 4

Students answer alone, then compare answers in pairs. Give feedback on answers with the group. Elicit or point out:

- that *issue* and *problem* are synonyms in this context
- the difference between *query* and *complaint*: something you don't understand vs. something you're not happy about. You can also point out that *query* can also be a verb and that you query something (not someone).
- that *query* is also sometimes used as a euphemism for complaint by businesses
- one or two ways that you can *get feedback*
- other expressions using the word *loyalty*: *loyalty card/ programme*.

Answers
1 make a complaint
2 report a problem
3 explain the issue
4 response time
5 customer loyalty
6 Customer Support
7 get feedback
8 offer a solution
9 have a query

PRONUNCIATION Ask students to group the following words from the exercise according to their main stress. Say the words aloud for them if they need a model.

Oo query, problem, feedback, issue, offer

oO report, complaint, support, response

Ooo customer, loyalty

oOo solution

Exercise 5
After the pairwork, get feedback by asking students to give examples of companies which offer particularly good and bad customer service. If they work for a company themselves, ask them how it could improve its customer service.

Further practice
If students need more practice, go to *Practice file 5* on page 114 of the *Student's Book*.

Exercise 6
Refer students to the list of words and ask them how many they know or recognize. If they don't recognize more than one, do the exercise as a group. Otherwise, ask them to do the exercise in pairs and then check answers with the group.

Answers
1 a discount
2 a replacement
3 a refund
4 a credit voucher
5 compensation

Exercise 7
▶ **5.1** After listening, ask the class for a show of hands on whether the experience was good or bad. If there is considerable disagreement, play the recording again. Ask them what information helped them to find the answer.

Answers
1st person: good experience   2nd person: bad experience

Exercise 8
▶ **5.1** Before listening again, refer students to the table. Ask them how much they can remember from the listening. Play the recording again and let them compare answers in pairs. Get whole-class feedback on answers, and ask them what they thought of the company's response in each situation.

Possible answers

	Situation 1	Situation 2
What was the problem?	It didn't talk.	It didn't connect to the Internet.
How did they contact the company?	by email	went back to the shop
How did the company respond to the problem?	They called back the same afternoon.	They said they couldn't help because the customer bought it online.
What solution did the company offer?	They sent a replacement and a £10 credit voucher.	They gave the phone number of the Technical Support hotline.

Exercise 9
Monitor the pairwork for correct use of the target language, and ask students to self-correct where necessary. Get feedback from the group by asking students to re-tell anything they heard that was particularly amusing, surprising, etc.

Photocopiable worksheet
Download and photocopy *Unit 5 Working with words worksheet* from the teacher resources in the *Online practice*.

Language at work

Exercise 1
Students work in pairs to make a list of reasons for online shopping before whole-class feedback. Make a note of any incorrect uses of comparative forms you hear to deal with later.

Possible answers
Online shopping is cheaper, easier than going to different shops, offers more choice of shops and products, more information about products.

Exercise 2
▶ **5.2** Students listen and compare their answers in pairs with the lists they made in **1**.

Answers
lower prices, flexible hours, possible to compare products online, number of products available, more information about the products

EXTRA ACTIVITY
Students can listen again and note how these numbers are said: 15,000, 15, 55, 24, 7, 11. With a strong group, don't give the numbers, but ask students to listen both for the numbers and how they are used.

Answers
fifteen thousand (shoppers)
fifteen (different parts of the world)
fifty-five % of people choose online shopping for lower prices
twenty-four (hours a day)
seven (days a week)
eleven % of people think this (better information) is a reason for buying online

Exercise 3

▶ **5.2** Get whole-class feedback after listening again.

Answers
1 cheapest
2 most
3 easy
4 wider
5 better

Exercise 4

You may need to explain the terms *comparative* and *superlative* (the first to compare just two things; the second to compare something with two or more other things).

Students do the exercise in the *Language point*. Go over the answers together. Check by asking them to work out, in pairs, the opposite of these comparative and superlative forms:

- *older* (newer or younger)
- *better* (worse)
- *the most dangerous* (the least dangerous or the safest)
- *more modern* (less modern or more traditional)
- *the easiest* (the most difficult)
- *quieter* (noisier).

The last adjective in the *Language point*, easy, will be an ideal opportunity to refer students to the *Tip*. Elicit or point out other two-syllable adjectives that end in -*y*, e.g. *angry, busy, happy, healthy, lucky, pretty, tasty*.

Answers
1 cheapest, wider
2 most expensive, less detailed
3 better
4 as

Two more useful rules that you might want to add:

- one-syllable adjectives ending in -*ed* are an exception to rule 1: they take *more* and *the most*. (e.g. *more tired, more bored*)
- *less* and *the least* are not used with short adjectives: we use *not as* … instead (*not as good, not as fast*).

Grammar reference

If students need more information, go to *Grammar reference* on page 115 of the *Student's Book*.

Exercise 5

▶ **5.3** Refer students to the question and elicit reasons for shopping in a physical store rather than online. Write their ideas on the board. Students listen to compare, and then check answers in pairs before whole-class feedback.

Answers
You get professional advice, the staff know more about the products, it's quick (you don't have to wait for a parcel to arrive), it's good to see and touch the products, it's easier to return or exchange items and doesn't cost anything. With online shopping, delivery times are longer and there's a risk of parcels being lost in the post.

Exercise 6

▶ **5.3** Students complete the sentences alone, and then check in pairs. They listen again to check the answers. As a follow-up, ask students if they agree with the ideas.

Answers
1 better
2 as low, quickest
3 most important, easier
4 less difficult, least expensive
5 as reliable, longer

Further practice

If students need more practice, go to *Practice file 5* on page 115 of the *Student's Book*.

Exercise 7

Before the pairwork, point out to students that their answer may depend on the product they're buying. If so, they should answer for different types of product.

Monitor the pairwork for correct use of comparatives and superlatives and ask students to self-correct if necessary.

Get feedback with the whole class by asking for a show of hands for each of the options suggested in questions 1–4, then inviting comments on the results of this survey.

> **EXTRA ACTIVITY**
> Give students a general knowledge challenge, e.g. *The Amazon river is longer than the Nile*. Ask them if it's true or false. Then ask them to write three general knowledge quick questions each. Give them five minutes. (Tell them they can use the Internet on their phones if they wish.) They then pair up with another pair and test each other.

Photocopiable worksheet

Download and photocopy *Unit 5 Language at work worksheet* from the teacher resources in the *Online practice*.

Practically speaking

Exercise 1

If students have difficulty understanding the word *soften*, tell them that the question is about situations where we have to be less direct and more diplomatic. Elicit answers from the whole class.

Possible answers
When you're talking to somebody in a position of authority, e.g. your boss, a customer.
When you think the other person will find it difficult to accept what you're saying, e.g. they may be angry or unhappy or not agree.

Exercise 2

▶ **5.4** Students listen, and then compare answers in pairs before whole-class feedback on answers.

Answers
The report isn't organized in the correct way. The employee has to redo the report and present the results by country.

Exercise 3

▶ **5.4** Play the recording once without stopping and ask students just to tick the expressions they hear. Then listen again and pause after each key sentence. Ask them to repeat exactly what the person said and identify who was speaking.

Answers
I'm afraid … B
Sorry, but … B
I'm sorry to say this, but … M
Sorry about that. E
Well, actually … M
… isn't very (+ *positive adjective*) M

Exercise 4

Students may need to hear the expressions used again. Play the recording again, or just say the key sentences aloud, as indicated in the Answers section below.

You might like to point out that we use the expressions *I'm afraid …* and *I'm sorry …* in any situation where we think the other person won't be happy with what we are saying. Refer students to other examples from the conversation: *I'm afraid I don't understand …*, *Sorry, but could you do it again?*

Answers
Complain:
I'm sorry to say this, but the report **isn't very** good.
I'm afraid they aren't organized in the right way.
It**'s not very** easy for me to use these statistics.
Respond to a complaint:
Sorry, but I thought that's what you wanted.
Sorry about that.
Correct wrong information:
Well, actually, I told you to present the results by country.

Exercise 5

Students practise the conversation. Allow them to refer to the audio script on page 148 of the *Student's Book* if necessary.

PRONUNCIATION Point out that softening your message is not only about the words, but also intonation. Play the conversation sentence by sentence, asking them to repeat with the same intonation. Then ask them to practise the whole conversation.

Exercise 6

Before going into role-play mode, discuss together how to use the expressions in **3** in each situation. The following words might be useful: *reliable, spellcheck*.

Monitor the pairwork for correct use of expressions and appropriate intonation.

Business communication

Exercise 1

Discuss the advice as a group or in pairs. Although it's standard advice for maintaining good customer relations, in certain cultures getting angry and immediately establishing responsibility for a mistake may be considered the quickest way to get what you want. Accept any alternative views without passing judgement.

Exercise 2

▶ **5.5** Play the conversations, pausing after each one to give students time to think about what they heard or to note answers. Let them compare answers in pairs, then play again as necessary. Get feedback on the answers.

Possible answers
1 The customer received the Spanish version of the book, not English. The customer will return the book. The supplier will send the correct version and credit the customer £5 to cover postage for the return.
2 The customer ordered a taxi for the airport but it hasn't arrived. The taxi company will call her back.
3 The customer's music system doesn't read MP3 files. It's been repaired once before for the same problem. The shop offers a replacement but not a refund.
4 The employee prepared the wrong files and will now prepare the right ones.

Exercise 3

▶ **5.5** Students can try to complete this exercise first in pairs, then listen to check. Get whole-class feedback. Check *look into it* (investigate the problem), *get back to you* (contact you again) and *right away* (immediately).

Answers
Conversation 1: sentences 2, 4, 8
Conversation 2: 6, 10
Conversation 3: 1, 7, 9
Conversation 4: 3, 5

Exercise 4

Remind students to refer to the information they noted in **2**. Recap on the main points if necessary. They should try and use all the sentences from **3**. Monitor the pairwork and make sure they are using appropriate language and intonation.

Further practice
If students need more practice, go to *Practice file 5* on page 114 of the *Student's Book*.

Exercise 5

Students may need help with vocabulary when talking about possible solutions. Get feedback on ideas with the whole class after the pairwork.

Exercise 6

Go through the *Key expressions* and make sure students understand how to use them. Check *I'm sorry for the inconvenience* (= the problem I have created for you) and *I'll wait to hear from you* (= receive more information from you).

For the first two conversations, ask them to prepare their roles in advance, thinking about which expressions they can use. For the last two, let them have the conversation spontaneously. Monitor conversations for correct expressions and intonation. If you hear a particularly successful (or amusing) conversation, ask the pair to repeat it to the group.

Photocopiable worksheet
Download and photocopy *Unit 5 Business communication worksheet* from the teacher resources in the *Online practice*.

Talking point

This *Talking point* has students in the role of judges deciding which company should receive an award. The basic premise, that of the WOW! Awards, is authentic, and the stories about the nominees are based on real-life case studies.

As a lead-in, ask the students to think of surprising or innovative ways in which a company could provide good service to their customers. Stress the 'wow' factor – something that makes a customer sit up and take notice! Then refer them to the text. Ask the following: *Who can be nominated?* (any company staff member) *Who does the nominating?* (customers) *Why do customers like to do this?* (as a way of saying 'thank you') Then ask students which story they like best, and why.

Discussion

Exercise 1

Discuss the question as a whole class.

Exercise 2

Students work in pairs to think of benefits for companies who do this, e.g. positive stories spreading word-of-mouth.

> **Possible answers**
> Good for the image of the company, even if they don't win. Makes all employees in the company focus on good customer service. Encourages customers to focus on positive aspect of relationship with company – not just negative (complaints) and builds customer loyalty.

Exercise 3

Students discuss their ideas in pairs, e.g. as a teacher, spending extra time after a class with a student who needs help, or having an 'extended' class with a group in a café.

PRE-WORK LEARNERS Students could choose a job they would like, or have had, and discuss how they or their company could 'wow' customers.

Exercise 4

Put students into the groups they'll be doing the *Task* in. They choose the most important criteria and add any others they can think of. Discuss their ideas as a class.

You might also like to ask if there are any possible negative consequences of participating in the WOW! Awards.

Task

Exercise 1

Groups of five would be best as there are five nominees for the award. Groups of three will work. Each student chooses a different employee to read about and tells their group. Encourage them to use their own words, by making notes as they read. It isn't necessary to read about each employee.

Exercise 2

In groups, students use the criteria from **4** to decide which of their employees will win the WOW! Award. Finish by asking each group to give their top three with a brief rationale.

ONE-TO-ONE You could choose, and read, two different employee nominations each. Use the criteria and discuss together which of each of your two employees is better, giving reasons. Then decide which of the two best candidates should win the WOW! Award.

Progress test

Download and photocopy *Unit 5 Progress test* and *Speaking test* from the teacher resources in the *Online practice*.

6 Employment

Context

Issues of *Employment* and human resources are of interest to everybody. All employees have to go through the recruitment process at least once in their professional lives, and often several times. They will be required to give a good account of themselves during interviews, and in international business environments these interviews will often be conducted at least partly in English. Candidates will also be interested in learning about benefits available at the company, including training possibilities. They will also want to understand something of the work culture, which can vary enormously from country to country and company to company.

In the first section of this unit, students will focus on the recruitment process, with particular reference to Internet-based recruitment. They will also have the opportunity to talk about their own experience of job-seeking and interviews. They will then learn the tenses necessary to talk about their own professional experience during a job interview, before focusing on ways to present themselves in the most positive way by avoiding negative answers.

The *Business communication* section focuses on the related employment issue of promotion. Students will practise some useful expressions for evaluating options during a meeting. In the *Talking point*, they will have the chance to compare the working cultures of two well-known companies in terms of the benefits they provide and to evaluate which of these benefits they would like to have in their own place of work.

Starting point

Let students consider the questions in pairs and then feed their ideas back to the whole class. For the first question, you may like to note their ideas on the board and then reach a consensus on the best of these.

Working with words

Exercise 1
Ask students to discuss this in pairs and then get feedback with the whole class. Alternatively, designate three areas of the classroom for each social network. Students 'visit' the areas according to their use of each one and discuss the question with others in the area.

Exercise 2
Students read and answer the questions individually before comparing answers in pairs. Check answers with the group.

> **Answers**
> 1 more than 400 million
> 2 To find jobs, people can put their profile on the website; look for friends or ex-colleagues who can maybe help them; answer job advertisements from companies looking for employees; get information about other people applying for the job.
> For employers, it's a good way to find employees because so many people use it.

Exercise 3
Students discuss the questions in pairs, then discuss ideas as a whole group.

> **Possible answers**
> 1 Yes – easier to find available jobs, and it's quicker and cheaper to apply online than to send by post
> 2 Probably more candidates, so more competition. Too much choice – you can spend a lot of time researching possible jobs.

Exercise 4
Students complete the stages of getting a job alone, then compare with a partner quickly before whole-class feedback. Check they understand the difference between qualifications, experience and skills by eliciting or giving examples.

> **Answers**
> 1 recruit
> 2 advertise
> 3 apply for
> 4 qualifications
> 5 experience
> 6 skills
> 7 reference
> 8 candidates
> 9 shortlist
> 10 interview

Exercise 5

Point out to students that the idea is to give their opinions
about the recruitment process based on their general
experience. (Note that they will be telling a specific job
application story when they get to **9**.) Students may need
help with words to describe their emotional reactions, such
as *stressed/stressful, nervous, relieved, excited, disappointed.*
After the pair discussion, get feedback from the whole class.

PRE-WORK LEARNERS If students have already experienced
applying for a job, ask them to share their ideas. If not, ask
them to think about the different stages and which would
be easier and more difficult (e.g. writing a CV, going for
interview, etc.).

Exercise 6

▶ **6.1** Students listen to two people talking about how
they got their job. Let them compare answers in pairs
before doing a whole-class check. The level of detail of their
answers will vary according to their listening ability, so don't
insist that they get every single detail before you go on to
the next exercise.

Possible answers

Speaker 1 only saw the advertisement at the last minute.
Because she was the last person to apply, she was the first
candidate that they looked at.
After a bad interview in one company, Speaker 2 went for a
drink and met an ex-teacher who needed technicians for his
own company.

Exercise 7

▶ **6.1** You could ask students to see how many words they
can complete in pairs before listening again. Listen and
let them check quickly with a partner before whole-class
feedback.

Answers

1 advertisement
2 application
3 qualified
4 shortlisted
5 interviewed
6 skilled
7 experienced
8 recruitment

Exercise 8

Draw a three-column table on the board with the headings
Noun, *Verb* and *Adjective*. Elicit the answer for the first
sentence (*advertisement, advertise*); ask students where the
words should go. Continue in the same way with the group
or have them work in pairs before feeding back on answers.
Check pronunciation and word stress of the different words.

Answers

qualification (noun), qualified (adjective)
shortlist (noun), shortlisted (adjective)
interview (noun), interviewed (adjective)
skill (noun), skilled (adjective)
experience (noun), experienced (adjective)
recruitment (noun), recruit (verb)

Further practice

If students need more practice, go to *Practice file 6* on page
116 of the *Student's Book*.

Exercise 9

Students work in pairs to talk about their current job.
Monitor and check for correct use of the target language.
Ask students to self-correct where necessary. Get feedback
with the group by asking if anybody went through an
unusual recruitment process. Students can answer for
themselves or their partner.

PRE-WORK LEARNERS Students could talk about a work
placement they did or the job of a person they know
(e.g. a friend, a relative).

Photocopiable worksheet

Download and photocopy *Unit 6 Working with words
worksheet* from the teacher resources in the *Online practice*.

Language at work

Exercise 1

Students discuss interview questions. Elicit ideas from the
whole class or let them discuss in pairs first.

Exercise 2

▶ **6.2** To check their understanding, ask students for
examples of non-profit organizations (e.g. the World Wild
Fund for Nature, Greenpeace, Save the Children). Students
then listen and compare answers in pairs before whole class
feedback.

Possible answer

She has work experience with three small organizations that
have operations in Africa. She has worked in Tanzania on the
construction of a new school.

Exercise 3

▶ **6.2** Students listen and underline the verb forms they
hear. Check answers with the whole class.

Answers
1 did you start
2 left
3 Have you ever worked
4 've never had
5 Have you been
6 've spent
7 did you do

Exercise 4

Check students recognize the tenses of each verb in **3** (if necessary refer them back to *Unit 3 Language at work*). Give them time to complete the explanations in the *Language point* alone or in pairs; then check answers with the class.

Refer students back to question 5 from **3** and ask if they notice anything strange about the choice of verbs in the two questions (the second one uses *been*, not *gone*). Refer them to the *Tip* for the explanation. Ask them to write sentences with *been* and *gone* based on their own experience, e.g. *I've been to England twice. My boss has gone to a meeting today.*

Answers
Sentences 1, 2, 7 are in the past simple. Sentences 3, 4, 5, 6 are in the present perfect.
1 present perfect
2 past simple
3 have(n't)
4 have, past participle

Grammar reference
If students need more information, go to *Grammar reference* on page 117 of the *Student's Book*.

Exercise 5

▶ **6.3** Elicit whether each question is about general experience or a specific time in the past. Then let students complete the questions in pairs before checking by listening.

Answers
2 How long did you stay there?
3 What other projects have you worked on?
4 Have you ever managed a team?
5 Why did you decide to work in this field?

Exercise 6

▶ **6.3** Ask students if they can remember Naomi's answers; then play the listening again. Check the answers quickly, then ask them to role-play the questions and answers. They could repeat the whole conversation with the roles reversed.

Possible answers
1 last year in March
2 four months
3 construction projects, and organization of training programmes
4 not yet
5 My mother lived in Africa when she was a child.

Further practice
If students need more practice, go to *Practice file 6* on page 117 of the *Student's Book*.

Exercise 7

Ask students to identify the tenses of the questions in the conversation (present perfect, then past simple) and to say why these are used (general experience; specific past time). Check they understand *ever* (in your life). Students then ask and answer the questions in pairs. Monitor for correct use of tenses and ask students to self-correct where necessary.

PRE-WORK LEARNERS Write the following cues on the board:

- go on holiday to an English-speaking country?
- learn any other languages?
- do IT training?
- play a musical instrument?

Exercise 8

Students who work in similar jobs could prepare the questions together in pairs. Alternatively, set this as homework and ask students to conduct the interviews next lesson. Tell students that not all questions have to be in the past simple or present perfect: questions using present tenses would also be quite natural in the context, e.g. *Do you have experience of XYZ? What are you working on at the moment?*

PRE-WORK LEARNERS Students imagine their future job and the questions they would be asked at the interview.

Exercise 9

Students interview each other. Monitor for correct use of tenses and ask students to self-correct. Note down three correct and three incorrect forms you hear, and ask students to correct them during final feedback with the whole class.

Photocopiable worksheet
Download and photocopy *Unit 6 Language at work worksheet* from the teacher resources in the *Online practice*.

Practically speaking

Exercise 1

Elicit answers from the whole class. Students from certain cultures may feel that there's nothing wrong with the employee's response, so refer them to the title of this section and ask why it's sometimes better to avoid a negative answer.

Possible answer
The employee's answer is quite negative or even impolite. The employee could explain why they've been busy and when the proposal will be ready.

Exercise 2

▶ **6.4** Students listen and decide what each conversation is about. They compare answers in pairs quickly and then get feedback with the group. What other details did they catch, e.g. *What documents in each case? What work experience?*

Answers
a Conversation 3
b Conversation 1
c Conversation 4
d Conversation 2

Exercise 3

▶ **6.4** Students listen to complete the responses. Pause the listening after each response to give students time to note down the missing words. Play each one a second time if necessary. Let them compare answers and discuss the follow-up question in pairs before doing whole-class feedback.

Answers
1 I saw a presentation
2 it's something I'd really like
3 I'll send it to you
4 I've often spoken it
All the information after *but* is positive. The speaker doesn't want to give a completely negative answer.

Exercise 4

Point out to students that it should be possible to give a 'no' answer to their questions. Elicit from or tell them how their questions could begin: *Do/Are/Did/Have/Could you …?*

Let them work on their questions individually. Ask them to make at least two questions for each situation. Monitor their questions and ask them to self-correct if necessary.

Exercise 5

Ask students to role-play all the 'boss' conversations first, and then the interview ones (or vice versa) so that they don't have to keep changing between situations. As a whole class follow-up, you might like to ask students for their 'best' questions from the list they made, then elicit different answers from around the class and vote for the best response.

Business communication

The language of evaluating options provides a natural context for practising comparisons, covered in *Unit 5 Language at work*. You could review this grammar point quickly first.

Exercise 1

This exercise allows students to reuse some of the vocabulary from *Working with words* in this unit. Students discuss the questions in pairs, then compare answers as a group.

Possible answers
1 need somebody with more experience or with special skills, nobody interested or right for post inside company, want younger people to join company (who are maybe cheaper!)
2 encourage good employees to stay with company, not necessary for other employees to get to know new manager, no additional recruitment costs

Exercise 2

▶ **6.5** Students listen and complete the table. If necessary, play the recording again, stopping at intervals to allow students to note the information. Students compare answers in pairs before getting feedback as a group. Ask the whole class for possible solutions to the problem.

Possible answers

	Arguments for	Arguments against
external	Can find somebody with more experience	Young engineers could leave company to work with competitors Not enough time to find the right person Cost of recruitment + high salary
internal	Company has young engineers who want to progress. Sends positive message. Can save money on recruitment	Young engineers don't have enough experience Japanese customer prefers to work with experienced managers

Possible solutions: recruit somebody from outside for the Japanese customer, but offer Project Manager training courses to younger engineers to keep them happy. Alternatively, use a more senior in-house project manager (if there is one) for the Japanese customer and promote a young engineer to do the work of the senior project manager.

Exercise 3

▶ **6.5** Students listen to match the sentences halves, then compare answers in pairs. Elicit or explain the meaning of potentially difficult terms, such as *I'd go for …* (I would choose), an *issue* (problem), a *key* advantage (important), *risky* (possibly dangerous) and *attractive* (interesting).

Answers
1 d 2 i 3 g 4 f 5 h 6 b 7 a 8 c 9 e

Exercise 4

Students read the suggestions and evaluate them. They should try to use as many of the expressions as possible from the *Key expressions*. Monitor the pairwork for correct use of these and ask students to self-correct as necessary.

Do whole-class feedback, asking different pairs to summarize their arguments for each point and see if the others agree.

Possible answers
1 Good to have more young people in the company and salaries will probably be lower, but you also need experienced people in the company.
2 Good to learn Chinese if the company is planning on working with China in future years, but could be a lot of money spent if only a few people will need it (or none at all).
3 Good to keep the experience in the company for a year to pass on information to new employees, and good for seniors who want to 'retire slowly'. But how many will want to stay for an extra year and how many will the company want to keep?

Further practice

If students need more practice, go to *Practice file 6* on page 116 of the *Student's Book*.

Exercise 5

Before doing this activity, ask students what training they have done – pre-work, within the company, outside or online. Students then read the three courses on offer and the descriptions of how they can be delivered, and decide which method(s) would be best for each course. They may decide to choose the same method for more than one course.

Ask students to work in groups of three or four. Monitor and help with any vocabulary. Then ask one person from each group to summarize the group's decisions and reasons.

ONE-TO-ONE Discuss briefly any experience the student has of face-to-face or online learning. Share your own experiences. Then read the three course topics and descriptions of the possible delivery methods, and ask the student to decide which would be best for each course and why.

Exercise 6

This activity allows further discussion on the theme of training, as well as further practice on the present perfect and past simple, as seen in *Language at work*.

Start by asking the whole class if they've had any of the types of training indicated. If the majority say yes, let them discuss in pairs. If most people haven't, then just ask the people who have had that experience to tell the rest of the class.

PRE-WORK LEARNERS Ask students to choose one of the courses listed in **5** and decide which they would like to do, in what format and why.

> ## Photocopiable worksheet
> Download and photocopy *Unit 6 Business communication worksheet* from the teacher resources in the *Online practice*.

Talking point

Discussion

Exercise 1

Before doing this exercise, ask students what attracted them to work for their present company. Ask pre-work learners how they chose where to study English or another subject.

Students read the two lists. Check *nap*, *hammock*, *laundry* and *pet*. Ask them to discuss in pairs which ideas they like most and why. Get feedback from the whole class.

Exercise 2

Students read the question and discuss it with a partner. Elicit their ideas.

> ### Possible answers
> Semco want responsible people who like their freedom but are capable of managing themselves. Google want young unmarried people who are still students at heart and are happy to work long hours while having fun.

Exercise 3

Students decide which company they would like to work for. Elicit some of their ideas, with reasons why.

Exercise 4

Students discuss what disadvantages there might be, e.g. employees don't go to any meetings.

> ### Possible answers
> Semco: some employees don't want so much responsibility – they just want to go to their office and be told what to do. Google: too much time spent at work and feeling that you have lost your freedom.

Task

Exercise 1

If students work for the same company, ask them to think about their own employer when choosing the advantages. If they work for different companies or are pre-work learners, they could imagine the company they all work for. To set the scene, ask them to agree first on the details of the company: area of activity, location of offices, number of staff, range of ages, etc. During the discussions, monitor and give encouragement and help with vocabulary where necessary. Students should each have a copy of their list for **2**.

Exercise 2

Re-pair the students to compare their lists. Monitor and make a note of any mistakes for future work; otherwise let students communicate freely without insisting on correct language.

ALTERNATIVE You could have each pair in the first phase representing either employees or management, in which case the benefits chosen may be influenced more by the roles they're playing. In the second phase, new pairs are then formed with each one having one representative from management and another from the employees.

> ## Progress test
> Download and photocopy *Unit 6 Progress test* and *Speaking test* from the teacher resources in the *Online practice*.

Viewpoint 2

Preview

The topic of this *Viewpoint* is *The customer journey*. In this *Viewpoint*, students begin by listening to people talking about choosing hotels. The students then watch and discuss a video interview with Dagmar Mühle from the Hilton Hotel chain. Finally, the students do a task which involves mapping a different customer journey.

Exercise 1

With books closed, ask students what criteria they bear in mind when booking a hotel. Then ask them to look at the criteria listed and to prioritize them. Students should first work alone, and then in pairs. You could then come up with a class list in order of preference.

Exercise 2

▶ **01** Students watch the video, and note down what each person considers when choosing hotels. If necessary, pause after each speaker to allow writing time.

Answers

Speaker 1	Speaker 2	Speaker 3
Location (in the centre) Canals / historic modes of travel	Location Good standard of hotel Opinion of other travellers (website reviews) Hotel facilities (swimming pool, restaurant)	Price Location Convenient to get to and from the airport Business facilities (meeting room, wi-fi, office space) Swimming pool

Exercise 3

Students compare their answers in pairs, and comment on how they relate to their own ideas from **1**.

Exercise 4

Students match the phrases from the interview they are going to watch with the correct definition. Do the first one together. Check the pronunciation of any words students find hard.

Answers

a 5 **b** 3 **c** 6 **d** 7 **e** 2 **f** 1 **g** 8 **h** 4

Exercise 5

▶ **02** Students read the numbers and phrases in the table, and then watch the interview with Dagmar Mühle: they should listen out for the information in the table and take notes about it. Students then share their ideas in pairs. If necessary, play the video again.

Students may ask for clarification of *ballroom* (n): a very large room used for dancing on formal occasions.

Suggested answers

3,600	Hotels around the world
10	Different brands
destination or brand?	Customers choose destination rather than brand.
facilities	Meetings and conference rooms, ballroom, 350 car park spaces
120	Countries around the world
loyalty programme	Hilton Honours, which gives incentives such as points and air miles

VIDEO SCRIPT

Hilton is the best known hotel brand name in the world. We have altogether about 3,600 hotels around the world and growing. We are divided into ten different brands – Waldorf Astoria, Conrad being the luxury; Hilton Hotels, Double Tree Hotels and Embassy Suite Hotels in the sort of mid-market segment and full service; and then more, the sort of limited service which is excellent products but not so much service, it's like the Hilton Garden Inns, the Hamptons, and these sort of brands.

How do customers choose a hotel?
I think a customer chooses destination more than brand, you know, to start off with. If anyone wants to come to London or to Düsseldorf or to Berlin, they may, you know look at the destination first and then they may look what's there and what's on offer and what hotels are there where they can stay.

How does the Hilton compete?
It is product, it's location, it's service, it's the different facilities in the hotel that we offer, for example we have a very good meetings and conference product and a ballroom which can seat a thousand people, we have 350 car parking spaces, so we are offering some unique features here. And, of course, service.
The fact that we are in so many different locations, I couldn't tell you now, but I think we are in over 120 countries around the world, so there are not many places where there is no Hilton branded hotel. Then we have a fantastic loyalty programme, our Hilton Honours, and that enables the regular user to collect points and air miles at the same time, so it's another incentive to stay and to sleep with Hilton rather than at the competition.

Exercise 6

Students discuss which hotel chains are famous in their own countries and what sort of customer goes to each one. They also discuss the various levels of service. Students could discuss this in pairs; then elicit some of their comments to the group. How do these chains compare with the Hilton?

Exercise 7

▶ **03** Before playing the second part of the interview, ask students to read the information in the table: they should then listen specifically for details relating to the customer journey, as well as how staff are trained for each stage.

Students check their answers in pairs, and then elicit their ideas to the group.

Suggested answers

Stages of the customer journey at the Hilton Hotel	Booking on the Internet or by phone, when they walk in and check in, interact with staff, the room, order room service, clothes in the laundry, sleep in the bed, a clean room, breakfast, the mini bar, use the conference facilities or meeting rooms, attend an event in town, use public transport, pay the bill, check out, receive a friendly goodbye.
Ways of training staff for each stage in the journey	1 Define the service standards. For example, answering the phone after three rings. 2 Introducing team members to their department and standards. 3 Check quality gets done.

VIDEO SCRIPT

What is the customer journey at the Hilton?

There are some basic areas that one expects, which is a nice welcome on arrival, a clean room and a comfortable bed, a good breakfast, and a friendly and helpful service.

We're looking at, at the customer journey, the customer journey is the path a guest takes when they arrive in the hotel, actually already when they make the reservation. So the customer journey starts perhaps in the Internet or the moment they are on the phone making a booking, and then it continues when they arrive, when they walk into the front door, when they check in, when they have the first interaction with the hotel staff on arrival. The next step is the room itself and what they do in the room. In the room they can, they can order room service, or they can, they can put clothes into the laundry or dry cleaning, they sleep in the bed obviously, the room is being cleaned every day. The next day they take breakfast, perhaps in the room or in the restaurant, they may use their mini bar, they may go, they may attend a conference in the hotel and use the meeting rooms in the business centre, or they attend an event in town and may use public transport. At some stage they will then leave again – they will come back to Reception, they will pay the bill and check out and hopefully receive a friendly goodbye and farewell and, you know, 'see you again soon'. So all that is the customer experience and the customer journey as we call it.

How do you train staff for a positive customer journey?

We have two ways of training our staff in customer service. The first step was to define our services and we call them service standards or brand standards. So a brand standard, for example, describes that the telephone has to be answered within three rings, that it has to be answered with 'Good morning, Dagmar speaking, Reception. How can I help you?'

The second step is then of course, the training we do with all the team members when they start. On day one they get an introduction to Hilton, and then they get an introduction into their department and the service standards of that respective department.

Number three is to check that it actually gets done, so twice a year we have mystery customers visiting us like a quality inspector, checking us and doing mystery quality control, to make sure that all the hotels and the hotel teams actually adhere to these service standards.

Exercise 8

You could discuss this as a class, or ask students to discuss in pairs the last time they stayed in a hotel. Encourage them to go through each stage of the customer journey.

Discuss ideas as a group, and find which stages were more or less successful and why.

Exercise 9

Students again work in pairs, but this time thinking about a different situation. Elicit other examples they could use. They should work together and note down each stage of the customer journey, and then note down what training staff would need at each stage. You could demonstrate this, perhaps in table format, on the board first, using one of the examples listed.

Exercise 10

Students then pair up with another pair to discuss their ideas on stages and staff training.

Exercise 11

Students should now consider the customer journey at their own company. You could pair same-company students together. They should list the key stages, staff training necessary, and then consider what improvements could be made.

PRE-WORK LEARNERS Students could discuss the 'customer journey' for new students at their school or college. Alternatively, they could think about a company they know well.

Exercise 12

Students from the same company could present their customer journey to the group in pairs, or individually.

Then, as a group, discuss which company currently offers the best customer journey!

Further video ideas

You can find a list of suggested ideas for how to use video in the class in the teacher resources in the *Online practice*.

Unit content

By the end of this unit, students will be able to

- talk about air travel
- discuss future plans, arrangements and decisions using *will*, *going to* and present continuous
- ask for and give directions
- make arrangements to meet.

Context

Travel is important to many business people – in the past it was only the top executives who travelled for work, but in today's global community, people at any level of an organization may find themselves being asked to travel abroad for a conference, a training session, or a meeting with customers or suppliers. Often they will have to make their own arrangements in advance, find their way around when they arrive and be prepared to make changes to their plans at short notice because of flight delays, cancelled appointments and other last-minute issues.

Not everybody has to travel, but many employees who don't travel are involved in liaising with future visitors to organize the details of their visit and making sure they are looked after during their stay.

In this unit, students will learn the vocabulary necessary to talk about air travel, whether in conversation at the airport during their trip or when talking about travel experiences. They will learn to use different future forms to talk about travel arrangements and to make travel-related decisions, as well as some expressions for making appointments. They will also practise how to ask for directions and be introduced to some stock phrases used when giving directions. Finally, they will play a game where they will be given further practice of a lot of the language taught in the unit.

Starting point

Note that here and in the *Working with words* section, questions have been worded so as not to alienate those students who either don't travel for business or have never been on a plane.

You could ask the students to discuss the questions in pairs first before eliciting a few ideas from the whole class.

Working with words

Exercise 1

Discuss the question with the whole class and ask them follow-up questions to get more details, e.g. *What additional costs might there be? Why are there often long waits at the airport? What's the problem with other passengers?*

> **EXTRA ACTIVITY**
> As a lead-in, you could ask students to work in pairs and make a list of advantages and disadvantages of travelling with low-cost airlines. After getting feedback on these, ask if they think the traveller complaints in **1** are particularly true for low-cost travel or for all air travel.

ALTERNATIVE If necessary, you could ask students to consider these issues for trains or buses.

Exercise 2

Check that students understand the word *annoying* in the title of the text. Then let them do the task individually before checking answers with the whole class.

> **Answers**
> 1 Uncomfortable seats
> 2 Additional costs
> 3 Long waits at the airport
> 4 Other passengers

Exercise 3

Students read and discuss the questions in pairs. Do whole-class feedback afterwards about their opinions on the subject. Elicit, if possible, students' real stories about airline complaints.

Exercise 4

Students do this individually, then check with a partner before whole-class feedback.

> **Answers**
> 1 weight restrictions
> 2 seat upgrade
> 3 delayed flight
> 4 aisle seat
> 5 hand baggage
> 6 self-service check-in
> 7 baggage allowances
> 8 airline charges
> 9 security scans
> 10 missed connection

PRONUNCIATION Check the sounds and word stress of the following: *aisle* /aɪl/; *upgrade* /'ʌpɡreɪd/; *baggage* /'bæɡɪdʒ/; *weight* /weɪt/; *security* /sɪˈkjʊərəti/. Note that the verb *upgrade* is stressed on the second syllable.

Point out that the words *baggage* and *luggage* are often used interchangeably. However, on websites, airlines usually refer to *baggage*, and you collect your suitcase(s) from the *baggage claim* area. When you buy a new suitcase, you're buying *luggage*, and customers often talk about their *luggage*.

Exercise 5

Let students discuss in pairs for two minutes, then elicit possible answers from the whole class.

Possible answers
1 Delayed flight and/or missed connection. Meeting has to be cancelled.
2 Children scared of flying or too noisy for other passengers. Parents really tired and stressed after journey.
3 Needs more luggage than the official allowance; has to pay excess baggage fees.

Exercise 6

▶ **7.1** Students read the three options, and then listen to the recording. Compare answers with the whole class, then write the following questions on the board and ask students to discuss the answers in pairs. Listen again if necessary.

• *Why will passenger 1 arrive late?*
• *What mistake did passenger 2 make?*
• *Why will passenger 3 have to pay more?*

Get feedback on answers with the whole group. Note that they don't have to understand all the detail of the conversations because they will listen again in more detail in **8**.

Answers
a Passenger 3 will have to pay more (because his baggage is too heavy).
b Passenger 2 made a mistake at check-in. (He only has three boarding passes for four people, and his suitcase is too big to take on the plane. He will have to go back to check-in.)
c Passenger 1 will arrive late. (The flight is cancelled because of a technical problem and she will arrive late in Amsterdam for her connecting flight to Stockholm.)

Exercise 7

Refer students to the *Tip* about compound words. Students may need help with the words *priority*, *hold*, *additional* and *extra*. Check answers with the whole class and ask *Wh*-questions to check their comprehension, e.g. *Who often has priority check-in? When do you get a free upgrade? What extra charges do airlines ask you to pay?*

Answers
2 passport
3 electronic
4 seat
5 airport
6 delayed

Ask students the difference between a *passenger plane* (a plane for passengers) and a *plane passenger* (a passenger on a plane). Then write the keyword *travel* on the board. Point out that *travel* can be a verb, but here they're going to use it as a noun. Then write these words around it: *first-class, agent, air, expenses, costs, long-distance, business, document, industry, rail*. Ask them to decide if the words go before or after the keyword, and to find the one word that can go before or after (*business*).

Point out that luggage you take on board with you onto the plane can also be called 'hand luggage' or 'cabin baggage' or, in the US, simply 'carry-on'.

Exercise 8

▶ **7.1** Pause the listening after each conversation to allow students to note down, then discuss, their answers. Then get feedback on answers with the whole class.

Possible answers
1 Her flight is cancelled, so she will miss her <u>connecting flight</u>. The airline offers her a <u>free upgrade</u>.
2 He used the <u>online check-in</u> but didn't print all the <u>boarding passes</u>. His suitcase is too big and he needs to check it as <u>hold baggage</u>. He can do this at <u>priority check-in</u>.
3 His bags are heavier than the <u>baggage allowance</u> and he has to pay <u>extra charges</u> for <u>excess baggage</u>. There are no <u>window seats</u> free – only <u>middle seats</u>.

EXTENSION Ask students their own experiences of some of these ideas when they have been travelling, e.g. a time when they missed a connecting flight, or travelling alone and having to sit in the middle seat.

Further practice

If students need more practice, go to *Practice file 7* on page 118 of the *Student's Book*.

Exercise 9

Students work in pairs, and choose one of the experiences to share and discuss. Encourage partners to ask questions to find out more information. Monitor the pairwork for correct use of the target vocabulary in this unit section and ask them to self-correct if necessary. Then ask the class if they heard any amusing or surprising stories from their partners and, if so, let them re-tell the anecdote to the class.

If you have students who don't have recent air travel experiences to talk about, write this (invented) newspaper headline on the board: 'New study shows 51% of business travellers now prefer the train.' Then ask students to work in pairs and discuss reasons why train travel would be preferable to air travel.

Photocopiable worksheet

Download and photocopy *Unit 7 Working with words worksheet* from the teacher resources in the *Online practice*.

Language at work

Exercise 1

Let students discuss the question briefly in pairs, then get feedback from the class. Write their ideas on the board, but without correcting anything that may be wrong yet.

Exercise 2

▶ 7.2 Students read the situation. Play the recording. Listen twice if necessary, pausing at intervals the second time. Let students compare answers in pairs before whole-class feedback.

> **Answers**
> 1 Emily is going to leave her company.
> 2 She's starting a Masters course in Psychology.
> 3 Fabrizio is arriving in Montreal.
> 4 He's leaving Montreal.
> 5 Fabrizio will call Emily again.

Exercise 3

Students underline the verbs in the extracts which refer to the future. Let students do this individually, then check answers with the whole class.

> **Answers**
> 1 'm going to leave
> 2 'm coming
> 3 'll call

Exercise 4

Students complete the *Language point* individually, then compare answers in pairs. Get feedback on the answers with the whole class. Point out how we can use the present continuous for talking about present actions (as seen in *Unit 2*) as well as for future plans. You could also explain that we often use *I'll …* when talking on the phone, because we are often making decisions as we speak, e.g. *I'll try again later/ hold on/give him the message/connect you.*

Refer students back to the sentences you wrote on the board in **1** and ask them to correct those that are wrong. If all the sentences were correct, ask students to explain why they used a specific tense.

> **Answers**
> 1 *going to* (I'm going to leave the company soon.)
> 2 *will* (I'll call you again on Friday.)
> 3 present continuous (I'm coming to Montreal for a conference next week.)

Grammar reference

If students need more information, go to *Grammar reference* on page 119 of the *Student's Book.*

Exercise 5

Before students work on this, point out that in some cases there is more than one answer. Ask the students to complete sentences a–f and then match sentences 1–6 with the responses in a–f. Let them compare answers in pairs before whole-class feedback.

> **Answers**
> 1 **b** is coming / is going to come, are showing / are going to show
> 2 **f** 'll do, 're leaving / 're going to leave
> 3 **d** 'll ask
> 4 **e** 're coming / 're going to come, 're staying / 're going to stay
> 5 **a** 'll change
> 6 **c** 'll send

Exercise 6

After students have practised the exchanges, you could ask them to do it again, but covering the responses. They then have to come up with responses that are similar, but not necessarily the same.

Exercise 7

Students work alone to read the text and underline the correct option. Then get feedback on the answers. Students will need to understand the details of the email for the activity that follows, so ask them to summarize what they know about Arianna Boyle's visit and what Meghan wants them to do.

> **Answers**
> 1 visit
> 2 She's
> 3 leaving
> 4 will
> 5 I'll call

Further practice

If students need more practice, go to *Practice file 7* on page 119 of the *Student's Book.*

Exercise 8

Refer students to the information files and ask them to read the schedule (Student A) and the email (Student B) respectively. When they exchange the information, you can either ask them not to look at each other's document but to take notes (more challenging) or to talk each other through with both documents in front of them (more natural). When they move on to point 2, point out that Arianna is coming to the town where they're studying or living, so they should choose activities for Arianna based on their local knowledge.

Monitor the pairwork for correct use of future tense forms.

When they have finished point 3, ask two or three pairs to summarize to the whole class what they have decided to do with Arianna.

> **EXTRA ACTIVITY**
> Find out which schedule students like best and why. Would they put together a different schedule for a different person?
>
> Then ask students to work in pairs to make a schedule for someone visiting their place of work or study. They should first decide who's visiting, and then put together a suitable schedule. They should consider how the person will travel from the airport, where they could take them for lunch, late afternoon and evening options, etc. In each case, they should be able to give reasons for their decisions. Students then present their schedule to the group. Encourage listeners to ask questions!

Photocopiable worksheet

Download and photocopy *Unit 7 Language at work worksheet* from the teacher resources in the *Online practice*.

Practically speaking

Exercise 1

If doing this after the previous section, you could use one of the places in the students' area mentioned in **8** and elicit possible ways from the class to ask for directions. Give immediate feedback on whether they are correct or not.

Exercise 2

▶ **7.3** Students read the sentences, and then listen to complete them. Let students compare answers in pairs before whole-class feedback. Play a second time if necessary, pausing at the end of each question. Point out how the verb comes at the end after *Do you know where …?*, i.e. not … *where is the nearest petrol station?*

Answers
1 Can you tell me
2 I'm looking for
3 How do I get to, Do you know where

Exercise 3

▶ **7.3** Students listen and number the directions. Let students compare answers in pairs after listening.

You may want to check potentially problematic terms like *traffic lights, roundabout, exit, corridor, stairs, motorway, signs.*

Answers
you'll see signs 8
on your right 5
take the third exit 2
take the first left 6
turn right at 1
in front of you 3
go straight on 7
go past the 9
then go down the stairs 4

Exercise 4

Students turn to the audio script on page 150, and practise the conversations. Encourage them to practise each conversation twice so each person gets to ask for and give directions three times.

Exercise 5

Be ready to provide extra vocabulary students may need for giving these directions and write these words or expressions on the board (with a drawing if possible) for the benefit of other pairs who might need them. You might like to encourage the students asking for directions to recap on the instructions they've been given, as we would often do in the real situation.

Business communication

Exercise 1

Students look at Fabrizio's schedule. They can discuss this in pairs, or you can elicit answers from the whole class. Make

sure they are using the present continuous and remind them about its use for future plans if necessary.

Possible answers
He's flying to Montreal for a conference on Sunday. He's arriving at 14.30. He's going to the IEFA conference from Monday to Wednesday (the Tuesday entry shows that the conference ends on that day at 5 p.m., so you should accept an answer of 'on Monday and Tuesday' as correct) and he's returning home on Wednesday evening.

Exercise 2

▶ **7.4** Before playing the recording, elicit when Fabrizio could be free to meet Emily. Then play the conversation. Let students compare answers in pairs before whole-class feedback.

Possible answers
1 Sunday isn't possible because Emily is flying to Toronto. Tuesday isn't possible because Fabrizio is having lunch with a customer and Emily isn't free in the evening.
2 They decide to meet on Wednesday at 1.15 p.m. outside the conference centre.

Exercise 3

▶ **7.4** Ask students to read the sentences. Can they remember any of the missing words? Then play the recording, stopping after each target sentence to allow students time to note and/or compare with a partner. Get feedback on answers with the whole class. Students may need clarification of these words and expressions:

- *When would suit you?* (When would be good for you?)
- *your availability* (the times you are free)
- *How/What about …?* (to suggest a day or time – no verb needed)
- *Let's meet …* (stronger suggestion than *How/What about …?*; used when you are quite sure the other person will accept)
- *… instead* (as an alternative to the last time I/we suggested)
- *I've got something on* (I'm not free, but I don't want or need to tell you why)
- *Shall we say …?* (normally used to decide on a specific time and place).

Refer students to the *Key expressions*. Ask them if there is anything extra listed (e.g. *That's fine for me.*).

Answers
1 Are you free
2 Can we find
3 would suit
4 What about
5 your availability
6 instead
7 got something on
8 work for you
9 Let's meet
10 Shall we say

PRONUNCIATION Refer students again to the *Key expressions*. Explain that with *Wh-* questions, the voice normally goes down at the end, and with Yes/No questions it goes up. Ask them to practise the questions with the appropriate up or down intonation.

Further practice

If students need more practice, go to *Practice file 7* on page 118 of the *Student's Book*.

Exercise 4

Students work in pairs and try to arrange a different time for Fabrizio to meet Emily. Monitor the pairwork for correct use of the target expressions.

> **Possible answers**
> Emily could cancel her engagement on Tuesday evening or maybe arrange to see Fabrizio on Monday evening if she's not back too late. The only other possibility is a quick meeting (over a drink?) after the conference before he goes to the airport on Wednesday evening.

EXTENSION For students who finish quickly, you could add another element by telling them that Emily now has a problem with the new time that's been decided. She now has to call Fabrizio back to rearrange again. Ask them to role-play this conversation.

Exercise 5

Put students in groups, of four to six if possible, as this will make it more difficult to find a time and will maximize the number of times they have to use the target language.

You could also participate in the lunch-date arrangements and thus help to prolong the conversations by deliberately being unavailable at times when the other students are free.

ONE-TO-ONE Ask your student to look at their calendar, with yours open too. If necessary, add in a few more events. Alternatively, you could each use a blank diary page for 'next week': add in six or seven events/engagements/meetings (e.g. out all day Wednesday; lunch meeting Thursday, etc.), without looking at each other's. Then try to fix a time to meet up for lunch.

Photocopiable worksheet

Download and photocopy *Unit 7 Business communication worksheet* from the teacher resources in the *Online practice*.

Talking point

The objective of this game is to practise the language for this unit, and reach Chris's office. Each pair will need a coin, and a counter or small object each.

Ask the students to read the instructions and study the board for a few moments. Check they understand the rules and the vocabulary. (The rules of the game are such that they will have to visit every square on their side of the board.) They both start in the top square at the 'airport': one student will go clockwise, the other anti-clockwise. Weaker students could be given time to prepare and rehearse the conversations mentally, but don't let them write anything down, as the idea of the game is to produce spontaneous speech. Check they understand *delayed*.

Monitor their conversations and make a note of any good language you hear, as well as any that needs correcting. Write up any vocabulary that students ask for help with so that the others can benefit from it too. Give feedback on the language they used, perhaps by writing it up on the board and asking them to correct any mistakes.

Progress test

Download and photocopy *Unit 7 Progress test* and *Speaking test* from the teacher resources in the *Online practice*.

8 Orders

Unit content

By the end of this unit, students will be able to
- talk about orders and deliveries
- talk about order processes using the passive
- discuss payment terms
- make and respond to requests.

Context

The success of a company depends very much on the effectiveness of their ordering and delivery processes. Companies are continuously looking at how to streamline their systems, and one direction which many companies are taking is online retailing. Although online purchases represent less than 10% of total sales worldwide, this area represents three quarters of total sales growth since 2015. Online retailers like Amazon have become leading figures in the retail of books, CDs and electrical goods. They have developed a fast and cost-effective order and delivery system which benefits both the retailer and the customer. Increasingly, we are also seeing cross-channel purchasing and delivery: more and more physical stores are selling through their own or other websites, and online retailers are offering delivery options to physical stores as an alternative to home delivery. In some countries, buying online is much more typical, e.g. 65% of Chinese shoppers shop online via their mobile at least once per month, while this figure is only 22% in the US.

This unit presents relevant language for talking about orders and deliveries. Students will also learn how to use the passive to talk about logistical processes in the present and past, and learn some useful expressions to talk about payment terms. In *Business communication*, they will practise making requests and asking for permission in the context of conversations about orders and delivery issues. In the *Talking point*, they will assess the advantages and disadvantages of different payment options and decide how they are going to sell a range of products of their choice.

Starting point

For the first question, elicit answers from the whole class. If students have access to the Internet, you might like to ask them to research 'best-selling products online' first. For questions 2 and 3, you could ask them to discuss in pairs first, before whole-class feedback.

Working with words

Exercise 1

Students read the questions. They could discuss them first in pairs. Discuss the answers with the whole class.

Possible answers
Valentine's Day: 14th February. The day you give presents to the person you love
New Year: 1st January, but Chinese New Year falls on the day of the new moon between 21st January and 20th February.
Diwali: The 'Festival of Lights' is a Hindu festival celebrated in autumn (northern hemisphere) or spring (southern).
Thanksgiving: Fourth Thursday in November. Started as a day to give thanks for a good harvest. Now most Americans' favourite holiday.
Mother's/Father's Day: Different dates in different countries. Children of all ages give presents to their parents.
Christmas: 25th December, Christian festival in which people exchange gifts. In many countries, presents are given on the evening of the 24th.
All these offer retailers the chance to sell merchandise (products) especially designed for these occasions, e.g. cards, gifts, special wrapping, flowers, magazines, recipes, books and much more.

EXTENSION Ask students what the most important commercial, and religious, holidays there are in their countries.

Exercise 2

Students read and answer questions individually before comparing answers in pairs. Do a quick whole-class feedback.

Possible answers
1 The last Friday in November. It's a big shopping day in the USA and other countries.
2 Retailers have had problems with stock and delivery because so many people ordered products at the same time.
3 Retailers need to have a better idea of the demand and employ more staff.

Exercise 3

Discuss the questions with the whole class. You might like to point out that Black Friday is a purely commercial day. Do students think it is better or worse than using a religious festival like Christmas for commercial purposes?

Exercise 4

Students do this individually, then compare answers in pairs before whole-class feedback.

Exercise 5

Ask students to do this in pairs before going over answers with the class.

Answers
1 quote
2 guarantee
3 process/place/deliver
4 check
5 transport
6 track
7 enquire
8 meet

Exercise 6

You could start by asking students to list the phrases in **5** in two columns under the headings 'Customer' and 'Supplier'. They then have to number them in a logical order and talk through the process at the same time. Check answers with the whole class.

Possible answer
First, the customer calls to enquire about a product. The supplier quotes a price, and the customer places an order. The supplier checks the product is in stock (or that he/she can meet the demand) and guarantees a delivery date. He/She processes the order and when it is ready, transports the goods to the customer. The customer can track the shipment online during this time. Finally, the supplier delivers the order to the customer.

Exercise 7

▶ **8.1** Students listen and answer the questions, then compare answers briefly in pairs. During the whole-class feedback, ask what action the supplier will take next (Conversation 1 – quote a price and place an order with the supplier if the customer accepts the price. Conversation 2 – check with the warehouse for a definite delivery date). Listen again if necessary.

Answers
a 2 b 1 c 1 d 2

Exercise 8

▶ **8.1** In pairs, students complete as many of these as possible. Then play the listening again, pausing after each target sentence to elicit the correct word. Ask them which of the words they completed are nouns and which are verbs.

Answers
1 enquiry (noun)
2 stock (verb)
3 order (verb)
4 quotation (noun)
5 guarantee (noun)
6 process (noun)
7 ship (verb)
8 delivery (noun)

Further practice

If students need more practice, go to *Practice file 8* on page 120 of the *Student's Book*.

Exercise 9

Refer students to the different bullet-point subjects and check they understand by asking them how the customer or supplier may talk about them, e.g. Stock: *Do you have them in stock? We don't stock that product.* Refer them to the *Tip* and ask them the difference between *shipping date* and *delivery date.* Point out that many goods are now no longer sent by 'ship', but that this word has been kept to describe the overall transport process.

Students use the conversation topics. Check the pronunciation of *antique* and *furniture*. Before they start, give them a few minutes to think about what they are going to say. Monitor the pairwork and ask students to self-correct if you hear incorrect use of the target language for this section.

Photocopiable worksheet

Download and photocopy *Unit 8 Working with words worksheet* from the teacher resources in the *Online practice*.

Language at work

Exercise 1

Students first make a list in pairs. Write their ideas on the board.

Possible answers
There's a mistake in the quotation; the factory has too many orders and can't produce in time; the goods are damaged when they arrive; the order arrives too late; the quantity is wrong; the transporter delivers to the wrong address.

Exercise 2

▶ **8.2** Students read the four descriptions, then listen to see what each conversation is about. Play the recording once and elicit the answers from the class. Ask them what words they remember that helped them to decide on the correct answer.

Answers
1 c 2 a

Exercise 3

▶ **8.2** In pairs, students choose what they think is the correct answer. Then play the listening again, pausing after each key sentence to elicit the correct answer.

Answers
1 is transferred
2 are shipped
3 are placed, guarantee
4 tracked, were delivered
5 was confirmed
6 was sent

Exercise 4

First, focus on the correct verb forms for sentences 1–6 in **3**. If students aren't sure of the passive/active distinction, point out one example of each in the sentences in **3**, then ask them to correctly identify the others. Then ask them to complete the explanations in the *Language point* individually, allowing them time to compare answers in pairs before whole-class feedback.

Answers

1 passive (Examples: sentences 1, 2, 3, 5)
2 active (Examples: sentence 3 *we guarantee,* sentence 4
   I tracked)
3 *is* (Examples: sentence 1, sentence 2, sentence 3 *are placed*)
4 *were* (Examples: sentence 4 *were delivered,* sentence 5,
   sentence 6)

PRONUNCIATION Highlight the weak forms of *are* /ə/, *was* /wəz/ and *were* /wə/ in the different passive forms in **3** (sentences 2 to 6). Point out that we pronounce them like this because they are not stressed in the sentence: the main stress falls on the main verb because it's more important. Ask students to repeat the sentences, providing a model if necessary. Then insist on correct pronunciation of these weak forms when students go through **5** and **6**.

Grammar reference

If students need more information, go to *Grammar reference* on page 121 of the *Student's Book.*

Exercise 5

Students do this individually, then compare answers in pairs before you check with the whole class.

Answers
1 are made, are sold
2 was sent
3 were checked
4 is guaranteed
5 was placed, were confirmed

Exercise 6

You could start by asking students to read through the text quickly without completing any of the verb forms and to tell you what 'Click and Collect' is. Have they used this type of service in their own country? Then remind students that for this exercise they have to choose either an active or a passive form. Ask them to work through the exercise in pairs, then do whole-class feedback.

Answers
1 is placed   7 opened
2 isn't delivered   8 were offered
3 is offered   9 were invited
4 choose (or are choosing) 10 were installed
5 was introduced   11 return
6 wanted   12 pick

Further practice

If students need more practice, go to *Practice file 8* on page 121 of the *Student's Book.*

Exercise 7

Encourage students to find at least one benefit and one disadvantage for the different people indicated. Monitor the pairwork and ask students to self-correct if you hear any incorrect active or passive forms. Get feedback on answers from the whole class.

Photocopiable worksheet

Download and photocopy *Unit 8 Language at work worksheet* from the teacher resources in the *Online practice.*

Practically speaking

Exercise 1

Elicit answers from the group and write them on the board.

Exercise 2

▶ **8.3** You may like to pre-teach the term *VAT* by asking students what the equivalent would be in their country. As an initial listening task, you could ask them which of the payment ideas from **1** were discussed in the conversation. Then listen again for the question asked here and let students compare answers in pairs before whole-class feedback.

Possible answer
The customer will pay €285 (€300 - 5%) immediately by bank transfer.

Exercise 3

▶ **8.3** Students complete the questions individually, then compare answers with a partner. They may need help with the terms *(to) charge, discount, instalments.* Only listen again at this point if necessary. Check answers with the whole class. You could then check their understanding of the questions by eliciting the answers to all the questions as heard in the listening (you may choose to listen again here).

Answers
1 total
2 include
3 charge
4 discount, advance
5 forms, accept
6 monthly

Exercise 4

Students complete the exercise individually before whole-class feedback.

Answers
1 c 2 a 3 b

> **DICTIONARY SKILLS**
> Point out that some words can be used as verbs and nouns, but with different word stress: when they are verbs, the stress is on the second syllable; as nouns, the stress is on the first syllable.
> *import, export, record, discount, refund, update, upgrade, increase, decrease, invite, present, reject, contract, object, subject*
> Students could use their dictionaries to see if the verb and noun meanings are similar (e.g. *import*), or very different (*object*).

Exercise 5

Make sure students understand they are playing the role of customer or salesperson for each situation. Encourage them to switch roles for the second conversation. With weaker classes, you may like to start by brainstorming the different questions the customer could ask in each situation. Monitor the pairwork and ask students to self-correct if necessary.

Business communication

Exercise 1

This initial exercise introduces the idea that the language we use to make a request will depend on what we are asking and who we are talking to. Elicit possible answers for each situation. If students can't come up with suitable expressions, give them a choice of two (e.g. *Do you think I could ask you to …?* and *Could you …?*) and ask them which they would use in each situation, and why.

Remind students that what you say depends on how big the request is and what your relationship is with the other person.

Exercise 2

▶ **8.4** Students read the instructions, and then listen to the three parts of the conversation. Listen twice if necessary, allowing students time to compare answers after each listening. Check answers with the whole class.

> **Possible answers**
> The man asks: for small change; if it's possible just to show his driving licence; for a bag.
> The shopkeeper asks the man: to wait (twice); for his confirmation email/order reference; for his ID; for a signature.

Exercise 3

▶ **8.4** You could ask students to try to match the questions and responses first, before playing the recording again. Then let students listen to check. You could pause the recording briefly after each request and response to allow students to complete the exercise. Then check the answers with the class. You may like to point out/elicit:

- why *No, not at all* is a positive answer here (it's in response to *Would you mind …?* which means *Is it a problem …?*)

- why the customer says the following: *Go ahead* (to give permission to serve the lady first); *I didn't realize* (The customer hadn't seen the other customer); *Here you are* (used when giving something to someone).

> **Answers**
> 1 f 2 h 3 a 4 c 5 e 6 g 7 d 8 b

Exercise 4

This exercise picks up on the distinctions highlighted in **1**. Do this as a whole-class exercise. You may like to start by creating a two-column table on the board under the headings 'simple requests' and 'less simple requests'. You will then add the different expressions to the table as you go through the exercise.

Elicit which three requests could be considered as 'simple' in the context of the conversations they've heard, i.e. the shopkeeper asking for the confirmation email, some ID and a signature. These are all normal requests in this situation and the response will usually be positive. Elicit/highlight which request expressions are used for these.

Then elicit or point out why the other requests are 'less simple' for the person talking, e.g. *Do you mind if I see this gentleman first?* (I'm asking you to wait your turn but I have to be polite), *Would you mind giving me some small change?* (I know shopkeepers don't always like to give change if you

aren't buying something). Highlight the expressions used here, too.

> **Answers**
> Simple requests: 3, 6, 7
> Less simple requests: 1, 2, 4, 5, 8

Exercise 5

Ask students to consider if the request is 'simple' or 'less simple' before choosing their expression. Let them work through all the situations with their partner, then ask a different pair to role-play each exchange to the whole class. If the other pairs chose different expressions, they can check with you if these were OK. Note that the request expressions chosen will depend in certain cases on the perception of the situation, e.g. you wouldn't use the same language when asking someone to open the window in your own office, and when in a railway carriage with four strangers. Let students justify their choice of language if necessary by explaining the context of their conversation.

| **Further practice**
| If students need more practice, go to *Practice file 8* on page 120 of the *Student's Book*.

Exercise 6

Refer students to the *Key expressions*. Ask them to read through. If necessary, check with them the response to *Would you mind …-ing …* and *Do you mind if …* in both negative and positive situations.

Stronger students could work on this in closed pairs first. Monitor the pairwork for correct and appropriate use of the target language. Then go over the whole conversation with the class by asking individual students to contribute a line to the conversation. Other students should listen to compare with their own conversations.

Weaker classes may need more help building up the conversation as a whole class first, before practising in pairs.

In either case, make sure that the pairs practise the conversation at least twice with each person playing both roles. They could swap partners to role-play it again.

| **Photocopiable worksheet**
| Download and photocopy *Unit 8 Business communication worksheet* from the teacher resources in the *Online practice*.

Talking point

Discussion

Exercise 1

As a lead-in, ask the class what payment methods they have used in the last week and what they have used them for. Then refer them to the questions and ask them to discuss their answers in pairs, thinking about both in-shop and online purchases. Get feedback from the whole class, focusing in particular on the 'Why?' question, as this will highlight the advantages and disadvantages from the consumer's point of view.

Exercise 2

▶ **8.5** Before listening, you could ask students what payment methods they think retailers would prefer – again making a distinction between in-shop and online sales. Then listen, twice if necessary, pausing after each speaker to allow students to note their answers. Let them compare answers in pairs before whole-class feedback.

Possible answers

	Payment type	Advantages	Disadvantages
1	mobile phone	nearly everyone has a mobile phone	not everybody has payment application on their phone, need to update regularly, problems with security
2	cash	no additional fees for shops; you have the money immediately	there are a lot of false banknotes; false banknote detector is expensive
3	contactless payment	makes high-street shopping for small purchases very quick and easy; no need to bother with coins, notes, or PIN numbers; the amount is limited	the limit can be annoying, but is a safety measure; some customers are worried that anyone could use their card if they lose it
4	credit card	people can pay quickly – don't think about the money they're spending	expensive – up to 5% per transaction
5	online	safe – payment not accepted if people don't have money in their account quick – immediate payment	high transaction fees

Exercise 3

This could be done as a whole-class activity or initially in pairs before whole-class feedback.

Task

To set up this activity, ask who in the class would be interested in setting up their own business one day. What products would they sell? You can then form pairs or small groups around the people with the product idea, thus ensuring that there is a leader in each group.

If students are short of ideas, you might like to ask them to research products of interest on a crowdfunding site like Kickstarter, where entrepreneurs try to get financial sponsors for their new venture. They can then use one of these products as if it were their own idea. If you don't have Internet access in your class, you can set this as a homework task and do the rest of the activity in the next lesson.

ONE-TO-ONE If your student isn't a potentially entrepreneurial type, you may prefer to research your own product idea in advance.

Exercise 1

Students work through the questions in pairs or groups. Give feedback on their ideas but don't focus on correcting their English unless their explanations aren't clear.

Exercise 2

Students present their ideas and then invite questions or suggestions from the rest of the class. You might like to ask students to vote for the best product and business plan.

Progress test

Download and photocopy *Unit 8 Progress test* and *Speaking test* from the teacher resources in the *Online practice*.

9 Selling

Unit content

By the end of this unit, students will be able to

- talk about advertising
- talk about obligation, necessity and permission
- interrupt and avoid being interrupted
- control the discussion in meetings.

Context

The world of advertising has been transformed fundamentally by the Internet revolution. To reach their target audiences, companies now have to advertise across an ever wider range of media as they seek to follow their existing or prospective customers in their increasingly diverse reading, listening and viewing habits. This has both advantages and disadvantages: it can make it easier to communicate a targeted advertising message at exactly the moment when a customer is thinking of buying. On the other hand, the choice of media is now so vast that a lot of careful thought and planning is needed to find the right mix – as well as a certain amount of luck. In addition, there is an inevitable backlash from many consumers fed up with the fact that advertising now follows us everywhere. For example, apps to block online ads on computers or phones are commonplace, and certain cities have moved to stop or limit outdoor advertising, as seen in the *Language in work* section of this unit.

This unit focuses first of all on the vocabulary of advertising and promotion. It then gives students the chance to talk about advertising laws around the world. *Practically speaking* and *Business communication* focus on useful expressions for asserting yourself in meetings, leading to a final role-played meeting where students decide on a promotional campaign. In the *Talking point*, they get to talk about the phenomenon of viral videos and plan a viral marketing video of their own.

Starting point

You could start by showing various advertisements on video or in magazines. Ask what they are for and if students think they work. Students discuss the questions in pairs or small groups before whole-class feedback. For the final statement, ask students if they think any of the controls on advertising are too strict / not strict enough in their country. You could refer them to the *Tip* on the second page of this unit section, as the terms *advertising* and *advertisement* will be used repeatedly throughout this unit section, so the differences and the abbreviated forms will be useful.

Working with words

Exercise 1

Students read the question and discuss it in pairs. Elicit answers from the whole class and write them on the board. You can then refer to this list when you get to **2**.

Exercise 2

Students read the text and compare answers in pairs before whole-class feedback. If you have Internet access, you could show students an advertisement for Orabrush and ask why they think the campaign was such a success. (The term 'viral video' may come up in conversation. Point out that they'll be looking at viral videos in more detail in the *Talking point*.)

Possible answers

The advice is to use social media, but to make sure that you choose the right media for your audience, to add value with special offers (this will get people talking) and to use humour.

Exercise 3

Students discuss the question in pairs, then share their ideas with the whole group. Students may come up with similar ideas to those in the 'Context' section at the beginning of the Teacher's Book notes to this unit. If not, you could feed them in to the discussion and ask students what they think.

PRE-WORK LEARNERS Ask students to think about a company they know something about and the different types of promotion they have seen before and since the use of the Internet.

Exercise 4

Students match the phrases and definitions individually, then compare answers in pairs. Follow up with whole-class feedback. You may like to elicit or point out the following:

- we generally use *advertising* when a company pays for it: we use *publicity* when it's free, or the company is mentioned in the media.
- the adjective from *awareness* is *aware*: *we are aware of a product* means we know that it exists
- *target* can also be a verb: we *target* a particular audience
- *boost* is similar to *increase* but is a faster action.

Some languages use the same word for *last* and *latest*. To test their understanding, ask what are the *last* and *latest* versions of a well-known product. *The latest* = the newest, most recent – up to now. *The last* implies nothing will follow, e.g. the last train (at night).

Answers
1 attract new business
2 boost sales
3 get free publicity
4 conduct an advertising campaign
5 word of mouth
6 reach a target audience
7 promote your latest range
8 increase awareness
9 offer discounts

Exercise 5

Students choose the correct word. Check their answers before students work in pairs to ask and answer the questions. Get feedback briefly with the whole class.

Answers
1 word of mouth
2 boost, sales
3 get free publicity
4 target audience, reach

Further practice

If students need more practice, go to *Practice file 9* on page 122 of the *Student's Book*.

Exercise 6

▶ 9.1 Before playing the recording, ask students how the three types of business mentioned advertise in their country. How did they choose their Internet service provider? Were they influenced by their advertising? Then listen and check answers with the whole class.

Answers
Office supplies 2
Health clubs 3
Internet service providers 1

Exercise 7

▶ 9.1 If you think students understood quite a lot the first time, let them try to answer the questions before listening again. Then play the recording again and let them compare answers in pairs before checking with the whole class.

Possible answers
Speaker 1: Everybody offers the same services for the same price. They are trying to attract sports lovers with a special offer for sports channels.
Speaker 2: People think they are expensive because it's a small independent shop. So they offer big discounts on 50 different products every month.
Speaker 3: They opened in a town where nobody knew them. They're offering a free month of classes to people who bring new customers.

Exercise 8

Before doing this exercise, refer students to the *Tip* on advertising. Remind them also about how this word is pronounced in its various forms: *ad<u>ver</u>tising*, *ad<u>ver</u>tisement* (US English), *advertise<u>ment</u>* (British English), *<u>ad</u>vert*.

Students then read the six forms of advertising. Check their understanding with questions, e.g. *What happens when you click on a click ad? What's the difference between a targeted and non-targeted email? What search engine do you use?* Students work in pairs and decide which forms they would recommend for the companies in **6**. Discuss ideas as a group, encouraging students to give reasons.

Possible answers
All methods could be used, however, the following might be best:
Office supplies: click ads, targeted emails, search engines
Health clubs: social media (connecting through 'friends'/contacts), click ads, advertising boards on location, search engines, promotional events, (to be able to offer something, and 'take a friend')
Internet service providers: social media, click ads, targeted emails, search engines (all online spaces)

Exercise 9

▶ 9.2 Students listen to the speakers describing how they advertise. Students compare answers in pairs before whole-class feedback. Ask them what they think of the methods.

Answers
Speaker 1: digital advertising boards at sports stadiums, click ads in online sports magazines
Speaker 2: targeted email campaign twice a year, getting website onto first page of search engine
Speaker 3: promote company on Facebook and Twitter. Free outdoor exercise class once a month in the summer

Exercise 10

If students are not aware of how their company advertises, they could either find this out for the next lesson or research another company as indicated below for pre-work learners.

Students discuss in pairs or groups, preferably with someone from a different company. Monitor for correct use of target language. Then, invite students to talk about any particularly interesting campaigns they heard about from other students.

PRE-WORK LEARNERS Ask your students to do some research outside the classroom: students research 'best advertising campaigns' on the Internet, then report on their findings in class.

Photocopiable worksheet

Download and photocopy *Unit 9 Working with words worksheet* from the teacher resources in the *Online practice*.

Language at work

Exercise 1

Students discuss the questions in pairs. Discuss as a group what kind of changes they talked about. Who thinks their town/city has changed for the better, or worse, and why?

Exercise 2

Students read the text, and compare answers in pairs. Ask them to vote on whether it's 'a good idea', 'not a bad idea', or 'not a good idea'; use this as the basis for a brief discussion. If most of them choose one of the first two options, ask how the city can compensate for the loss in advertising revenue.

Exercise 3

Students match the verbs in bold to the correct meaning, and then compare with a partner. Check with the whole class. Note that in certain languages the 'not possible' and 'not necessary' notions are often expressed with the same verb, so it's important to make the distinction clear between *don't have to / don't need to* and *can't / aren't allowed to*. Note that two gaps at the end of the *Language point* don't have a verb in the text. Students discuss what verbs would fit there.

Answers
1 have to / need to
2 don't need to
3 can / (are allowed to)
4 aren't allowed to / (can't)
The two missing verbs are 'are allowed to' and 'can't'.

Grammar reference

If students need more information, go to *Grammar reference* on page 123 of the *Student's Book*.

Exercise 4

▶ **9.3** Students listen to people discussing advertising. Check answers quickly as a group. Don't listen again at this stage.

Answers
a 3 b 4 c 1 d 2

Exercise 5

▶ **9.3** Students try to complete the sentences with verbs from **3**. Point out to students that even if they don't remember the verbs from the listening, they can complete these sentences in a logical way. Students complete the sentences individually, then compare answers in pairs. Listen again to check answers with the whole class, pausing after each target sentence.

For the second part of the task, students need to refer more to the general point that each speaker is making, rather than the individual sentences (sentences 5–8 are facts, not opinions, so it's difficult to respond to them). You could refer students back to the statements in **4** and ask them why each speaker has that opinion e.g. *Statement c: Outdoor advertising isn't attractive because billboards look unattractive and get bigger every year.* Play the recording again if necessary. They could discuss their opinions as a group, or in pairs first.

Answers
1 have to
2 don't need to
3 need to
4 have to
5 aren't allowed to
6 are allowed to, can't
7 don't have to
8 can
9 don't have to

ALTERNATIVE You may prefer to move straight on to the controlled practice in **6**. You could then come back to this part before the final exercise.

Exercise 6

Students read the messages and complete the task in pairs before whole-class feedback. They may need help with the following: *throughout the store*, *non-refundable* (NB they learnt *refund* in *Unit 5*), *cancellation insurance* (they learnt *cancelled flight* in *Unit 7*), *bill posters* and *prosecuted*.

Suggested answers
2 You can get a 30% discount, but you have to buy today.
3 You aren't allowed to pay by cheque. You have to pay cash or by card.
4 You don't have to pay for delivery if you spend more than €100.
5 You can't have a refund for this ticket. If you want to be protected, you have to take cancellation insurance.
6 You aren't allowed to / can't advertise here.

Further practice

If students need more practice, go to *Practice file 9* on page 123 of the *Student's Book*.

Exercise 7

Students read the instructions. Check the vocabulary. They should spend a few minutes thinking which question form is most appropriate for each item. Point out the formation of the questions (students may want to say **Have you to …?*); drill a few examples if necessary. Students work in pairs to answer the questions. Encourage use of the modal verbs from **2**.

ALTERNATIVE If students are from the same country, ask them to research a different country online and to report back on what they find out.

> **EXTRA ACTIVITY**
> If you think students need more practice in this area, ask them to discuss other rules and regulations in their countries. Topics could include: laws for under-18s, voting and elections, driving (both cars and motorcycles), drinking alcohol, travelling to other countries / visas. NB Make sure you choose topics which are acceptable in your local teaching context.

Photocopiable worksheet

Download and photocopy *Unit 9 Language at work worksheet* from the teacher resources in the *Online practice*.

Practically speaking

Exercise 1

▶ **9.4** As a lead-in, ask the class why it is sometimes necessary to interrupt somebody who is speaking. When is it impolite to do this?

Play the recording and let students compare answers in pairs before whole-class feedback. Students familiar with Internet advertising and the use of cookies may give more detailed answers, and their opinions on the subject. For others, accept minimal answers and move on to the next exercise.

Suggested answers
1 They're talking about targeted advertising on the Internet and 'cookies'.
2 They don't agree.

Exercise 2

▶ **9.4** Students listen and number the phrases. Check answers quickly with the whole class after listening.

Answers
a 4 b 5 c 3 d 2 e 1

Exercise 3

Do this activity with the whole class. Play the recording again if necessary to allow students to hear the expressions in context, pausing after each expression is used.

Answers
1 a,e 2 b,d 3 c

Exercise 4

Each pair chooses the same subject to talk about. Give them enough time to think individually of three or four ideas so that the discussion goes on long enough for them to use the phrases from **3**. They may tend to let each other finish without interrupting: encourage them to interrupt as often as possible, even if it means being a little impolite. Model this first with a stronger student, with the teacher interrupting.

ALTERNATIVE You may like to introduce a game element by telling students to give themselves a point each time they use one of the target expressions.

Business communication

EXTRA ACTIVITY
Ask students what they like and/or dislike about meetings. Elicit problems that business people often have about meetings (too long, not focused enough, some participants talk too much) and explain that controlling the discussion (the focus of this section) is an important skill, as it can reduce these problems.

PRE-WORK LEARNERS Ask the students what they think the problems might be with meetings in companies.

Exercise 1

▶ **9.5** Due to length, you could break the listening into three sections and ask students to compare answers after each section. Students listen to complete the notes. Get feedback at the end with the whole class.

Answers
Advertising:
Money spent last year: €28.6 million
Budget this year: €37.5 million
Extra money to be used for: big social media campaign
Sales:
This year: 7 % increase
Next two years: 7 %
Key markets: the Czech Republic, Poland, Hungary
Action:
Edward to prepare detailed sales forecast
Anton to provide details of social media campaign

Exercise 2

▶ **9.5** You may need to explain or elicit the meanings of sentences 1–6 before students can match them with a–f. In particular, they may not understand the following terms:

- *catch* = hear
- *get off the subject* = talk about a different subject
- *cover* = deal with
- *I'm not with you* = I don't understand what you mean
- *sum up* = describe the main points
- *be more specific* = give more detail
- *move on (to)* = change (to a new subject)
- *come back to* = return to (a subject discussed before).

Students match A and B individually, then compare answers in pairs. Play the recording again and pause after each matched pair of sentences to elicit the correct answers.

Answers
1 f 2 c 3 e 4 d 5 b 6 a

Refer students to the *Key expressions*, and check they understand the phrases.

PRONUNCIATION Ask students to mark the main stressed words on the follow-up sentences a–f (and stressed syllables in the case of words with more than one syllable).

Answers
a Can we <u>sum</u> up what we've a<u>greed</u>?
b Could you be more spe<u>cif</u>ic?
c What was the <u>last</u> figure?
d Can we <u>move</u> on to the <u>next</u> point?
e Can we come <u>back</u> to that <u>lat</u>er?
f We <u>need</u> to discuss our new <u>mar</u>keting campaign.

Exercise 3

Students use the sentences as prompts. Encourage pairs to come up with alternative responses in each case. Get feedback on different possible answers with the whole class.

Possible answers
2 Sorry, I'm not with you. Can you be more specific? Do you want to recruit more people?
3 We're getting off the subject. Can we come back to that later if we have time?
4 Sorry, I didn't catch that. What was the second figure?
5 No, I think we've covered recruitment. Can we move on to the next point?
6 No, I think that's everything. Can we sum up what we've agreed?

Further practice

If students need more practice, go to *Practice file 9* on page 122 of the *Student's Book*.

Exercise 4

Refer students to the meeting agenda. If you have at least four students in your class, ask them to prepare for the meeting in pairs by discussing their reactions to the proposals and thinking of ideas for the advertising campaign.

Form meeting groups of four to six students. Divide large groups into separate meetings. Don't appoint a chairperson: the idea is that everyone can control the discussion.

Monitor for correct use of the sentences from this section, including natural stress, rhythm and intonation. Stronger groups could be encouraged to include interrupting language from the *Practically speaking* section of this unit: a quick recap of the expressions will be useful before starting.

Bring common mistakes to the students' attention at the end of the meeting and ask them to self-correct.

With several groups, ask each group to summarize at the end.

ONE-TO-ONE This activity works perfectly well as a two-person discussion, but in your preparation, you could include some information which will prompt the student to use the target language for this section, e.g. some (invented) statistics which they will have to ask you to repeat, some deliberately unclear arguments or a deliberate digression. Avoid being the unofficial chairperson: let the student move things along.

Photocopiable worksheet
Download and photocopy *Unit 9 Business communication worksheet* from the teacher resources in the *Online practice*.

Talking point

Discussion

Exercise 1
As a lead-in, ask students why some videos on YouTube get fewer than a hundred views, and others several million. Write their ideas on the board. Students then read the five tips; ask them which of the ideas mentioned are similar to their own. Deal with any vocabulary problems in the text.

> **Possible answers**
> Similar: traditional and online adverts are both short; people talk about good advertisements; need to interest the viewer straight away.
> Different: people often share online videos with friends; people are more likely to close an online video before it finishes, but are more likely to watch a TV ad until the end. Online adverts can encourage you to click, and go to a site, or take action.

ALTERNATIVE As an alternative lead-in, tell students they are going to answer two questions: *What is a viral video? Why do you think some videos 'go viral'?* Then ask them to type in the terms 'top viral videos' and 'top viral marketing videos' on YouTube and to watch a selection from each to give them an idea of how to answer the two questions. If you have no Internet access, this could be done in advance at home.

Exercise 2
Students discuss in pairs which tips they think are more or less important. Encourage alternative ideas.

Exercise 3
Students discuss what sorts of videos they share. In feedback, you could ask them to give reasons.

Task

Exercise 1
Divide students into groups of three or four. Ask them to think about what company they are going to plan for. When they've made their choice, note them all on the board.

ONE-TO-ONE Ask the student to decide which company they want to focus on, and what the video will be about. Discuss their ideas, and suggest some of your own. If the student is self-motivated, they could do this task at home, and then present it to you next lesson.

Exercise 2
Students decide on a subject for their video.

Exercise 3
Students discuss which of the five tips they will follow.

Exercise 4
Students plan their video together, and give timings. Encourage them to map it out on paper like a story board.

Monitor and give help with vocabulary or ideas. Don't correct their use of language unless it's not clear to the other students, but make a note for later work.

Exercise 5
Each group chooses a spokesperson to present their video plan to the rest of the class. Encourage listeners to give feedback, e.g. on an idea they particularly like or any suggestions they have.

Progress test
Download and photocopy *Unit 9 Progress test* and *Speaking test* from the teacher resources in the *Online practice*.

Viewpoint 3

Preview

The topic of this *Viewpoint* is *company logos*. In this *Viewpoint*, students begin by listening to people explaining why company logos are important, then watch a video which examines the role colour plays in the design of logos, before finally designing a new logo themselves.

Exercise 1

You could start by showing, or drawing on the board, one or two famous logos, and asking students to guess what company they represent. Students then discuss in pairs what famous logos they know, and how important they think a logo is. Ask them to show, if possible, and discuss their company or college logo, in terms of colour and design, and what it may represent.

Exercise 2

▶ 01 Give students time to read the information in the table, and then play the video. Ask students to make notes in the table. Reassure students that they do not need to understand all of what the speakers say, but to try to pick out their key points only.

Note that speaker two (Mark) does not answer the third question.

Ask students if either speakers' comments or opinions are similar to their own. Discuss as a group.

Possible answers

	Speaker 1	Speaker 2
What do you think makes a good logo?	Typeface (font) has to represent look, tone and feel that you want to create for/with your company. It can be (make it) formal, fun, less serious. Design (mark) which is symbolic or metaphorical or an immediate read for what your company stands for is very powerful.	A quick understanding at a quick glance of what the company is about. Something that you can immediately recognize on a van that passes you on the street. Something that sticks in your head.
Can you tell us about your company logo?	The company (Vantiv) does not have a design mark, so the logo is only words. Stylized with a particular font, all lower case, grey. Trademarked.	The company (Lincoln college) has a crest: three reindeer, a shield and three stars (diamonds) and a little star.
How important is colour in a logo?	Very powerful. Red can be aggressive and blue is associated with finance and is considered safe.	

Exercise 3

Students read the words for talking about logos, and put them into the categories. Do the first word together.

Answers
How it looks: small, modern, round, bright
Where you see it: van, website, supermarket, packaging
How it makes you feel: optimistic, excited, happy, safe

EXTENSION Ask students which words they could use to describe their own company or college logo.

Exercise 4

Students work in pairs and look at the colours. Ask them to suggest which types of businesses use which colour. Elicit one or two to get them started (e.g. car manufacturers, drinks companies, etc.).

Exercise 5

▶ 02 Before playing the video, ask students to read the information in the table so that they know what to listen out for. Then play the video. If necessary, play it a second time, pausing after each colour section.

Students check their answers with a partner, and then check the answers together.

Answers
1 happy
2 Red
3 good
4 IT
5 car companies
6 Internet search engine

VIDEO SCRIPT

They're all around us. We see them every day.
On cars.
On packaging.
On the sides of vans.
On the front of our local shops.
On the shelves of our shops.
In our homes.
On our phones.
We even wear them!
Logos are everywhere.
So what makes a logo powerful?
Colour is a key factor.
Colours send a message and create an emotional response. Colour also says something about our business. Let's take a look at some logos to see how they use colour.
For most people, yellow is a bright and optimistic colour. It makes us feel warm and happy inside. So brands like fast food restaurants use yellow on their signs and logos. It says to customers: 'Hey! We're a happy place to bring the kids and have fun'.
Another colour that's popular with fast food restaurants is red. Red is an exciting colour which you often see on burger bars but of course …
Red can also mean danger or there's an emergency, so you'll see red logos for medical companies.
Of course, you can use colour in a logo to say something completely different about a product. For example, imagine you

are selling a soft fizzy drink. You'd probably have a red logo to let everyone know how exciting life becomes when you drink this product.

But what happens when everyone wants a fizzy drink with less sugar in and you have to make your product healthier? Simple. Just turn your red logo into a green logo. After all, green sends the message that the product is clean and good for you.

So green is also good if you're an energy company, or maybe sell organic food. Another colour that's healthy is blue. Now earlier we said that logos for medical companies are often red. That's usually when they are involved with first aid or emergencies. But we associate blue with safety and reliability so blue is popular with the pharmaceutical industry and with IT businesses.

You might think blue is a bit boring, but even less exciting than blue is the colour grey. Who uses grey as a logo?

Brands that produce technology use grey to emphasise how reliable their products are.

A classic timeless grey or silver logo is also the choice of many car companies because it represents strength and performance.

But what if you want your product to say your company is many things to many different people? Maybe you're an Internet search engine that everyone uses.

The answer is simple.

Think about it. What does your company logo say about you and your business?

EXTENSION Ask students if their company or college logo fits into the colour categories described.

Exercise 6

▶ 02 Before playing the video again, ask students to read the sentences and check their answers with a partner. Then play the video again. Students check their answers again, then check them with the whole class.

Answers
1 makes, feel
2 says
3 mean
4 sends, message
5 good
6 associate, popular
7 represents

Exercise 7

You could deal with these questions in two stages, as each one could promote a lot of discussion.

Give students time to read the questions, and perhaps make a few notes, and then pair them off with a new partner to discuss the questions.

Discuss a few of their ideas as a group, and find out how closely the logos they know resemble the information in the video (in the table in **5**), or whether there are significant differences.

Exercise 8

Students work in small groups. They should imagine that they are going to design a logo for each of three companies. If you are short of time, each group could focus on just one of the companies.

Tell them first to look at the pictures, and descriptions, so that they understand a bit about each company. Then give them time to discuss the logo and draw a sketch.

They should use the information in **5** to help and give them ideas.

ONE-TO-ONE The same exercise can be used with a one-to-one student. If time is an issue, you could ask the student to choose just one logo to design.

Exercise 9

Students present their ideas to the class. Remind them before they start to use the phrases from **6** to help.

Invite feedback from other class members on the suitability of the colours chosen and the design, and how the logo would make them feel, as customers.

EXTENSION Students could find similar companies online in their own time and compare those logos with the ones they designed.

Further video ideas

You can find a list of suggested ideas for how to use video in the class in the teacher resources in the *Online practice*.

10 Environment

Unit content

By the end of this unit, students will be able to

- talk about environmental protection
- talk about probable future results
- ask for clarification
- give a formal presentation.

Context

The topic of *Environment* will be relevant to all business people. Leaders and managers now realize that financial and public relations benefit from a much greener approach to business, so most companies, both large and small, now usually address their environmental credentials. Partly this is because consumers are less and less inclined to use a company which has a reputation for being anti-green, so a company will lose business unless it can show it is environmentally-friendly. If you type 'making business green' into an Internet search engine, you will get around a billion hits.

To some extent, our attitude to green issues is cultural. For example, northern European countries such as Germany or Denmark have traditionally been at the forefront of making business green; developing countries have taken the understandable viewpoint that restrictions on output or distribution are going to hit them hard just as they are gaining market share. So your students are likely to express differing viewpoints, depending on where they come from and what business they are in.

This unit provides the opportunity to discuss environmental issues within the business world and to learn useful vocabulary in that field. It also gives a basic introduction to the language of presentations and gives students ample chance to practise. They will also practise asking for clarification. The unit ends with a *Talking point* where students discuss ways of getting people to change their habits for the better to benefit themselves, and/or others, and make a short presentation.

Starting point

Elicit ideas for 1 from the whole class, then ask them to discuss 2 in pairs. Before answering 2, you could brainstorm a list of problems on the board, and then ask students to put them in order of urgency. Check the pronunciation (including stress) of *environment*: /ɪnˈvaɪrənmənt/ and *environmental* /ɪnˌvaɪrənˈmentl/.

Working with words

Exercise 1

Ask students what information they can think of which is stored on computers, e.g. personal and public data, files, etc. Then ask them to work in pairs to answer the questions. Elicit a few ideas briefly from the whole class.

> **Suggested answers**
> 1 Personal data; corporate (from companies) data; government data.
> 2 It is usually stored on huge servers (main computers which connect several computers connected in a network).
> 3 They require a lot of energy, and could be costly to produce and run.

Exercise 2

Students read the text, compare their answers in **1** and answer the question.

Check students understand *generate* (v) – to produce or create sth; *(bomb)* /bɒm/ *shelter* (n) – a place of protection from rain, danger or attack; *extract* (v) – to remove or obtain a substance from sth., e.g. by using an industrial or a chemical process.

> **Answers**
> In Helsinki, the servers are kept cool under water in the Baltic Sea, and the heated water is then used to heat homes.
> At Google, the energy for big data servers comes from windfarms.

Exercise 3

Students work in pairs and discuss the questions.

EXTENSION Ask students if these ideas could be implemented in their own countries, or companies, and how.

Exercise 4

Students work individually, then compare answers in pairs. Check answers with the whole class.

Point out that we sometimes use *reuse* and *recycle* interchangeably. Note that *re-* is a prefix meaning 'again' on the following words: *reuse, recycle, renew,* but not on *reduce.*

Exercise 5

After students have done the exercise in pairs, encourage them to develop their answers by using one each of the other verb-noun combinations in a sentence about themselves or their working/study environment.

DICTIONARY SKILLS

Some students (e.g. French-speaking) may confuse the meaning or spelling of the following: *consumption, customer, custom, costume.*

You could suggest they check their dictionaries to check the meaning, as well as to find other words in the word families, e.g. *consume* (v), *consumer* (n, person), *consumption* (n, object). Suggest they also check which part of the word is stressed, i.e. con<u>su</u>mer but <u>cust</u>omer.

EXTRA ACTIVITY

Ask students to work in pairs and write down two verb–noun combinations they want to remember. They should then write down an example when they would do this, or this would happen, but without using the phrase, e.g. *My brother cycles to work every day because he doesn't want to …* (pollute the environment); *We have three big boxes in a cupboard in the kitchen to … We put empty containers and packaging in them, and then we take it all to a general collection point.* (recycle paper/plastic/glass)

Give students five minutes to prepare their situations, and then ask them to pair up with another pair. Each pair reads out one of their situations and the other pair tries to guess which verb-noun combination it refers to.

Exercise 6

▶ **10.1** Tell students they will hear four short extracts that correspond to the four pictures. Let students compare answers in pairs, then check with the whole class.

Exercise 7

▶ **10.1** Students work in pairs and listen again to note which verb-noun combinations in **5** are used. You could suggest they tick them off as they hear them. Check the answers with the whole class.

Further practice

If students need more practice, go to *Practice file 10* on page 124 of the *Student's Book.*

Exercise 8

Students discuss the four initiatives. Ask if any of them are in place in their own places of work or study, and/or whether they would be feasible. What might the disadvantages be of each?

Exercise 9

Students should form pairs from different companies if possible, and find out what their partner's company does.

PRE-WORK LEARNERS   For questions 1 and 2, students should discuss their place of study. They could write a letter to their principal, suggesting new green initiatives the school could take.

Refer students to the *Tip* about the word *green.* Can they use it to describe their place of work or study, product or service, or one they know?

Photocopiable worksheet

Download and photocopy *Unit 10 Working with words worksheet* from the teacher resources in the *Online practice.*

Language at work

Exercise 1

Students answer the questions in pairs. Elicit a few ideas from the whole class, asking them to give reasons.

Exercise 2

▶ **10.2** Tell students they are going to hear a discussion about the costs of trams and electric buses, as well as how many passengers each can carry. Ask them to listen for the numbers and complete the table.

Write the table on the board. Ask the students for their responses and fill in the table.

Ask students if they have changed their mind about which idea they prefer, and if so, why.

Exercise 3

▶ **10.2** Students underline the correct word individually, then compare answers in pairs. Then play the recording again for them to check. Confirm the answers with the whole class.

Answers
1 choose, will be
2 will cost, have to
3 don't, won't
4 will, loses

Exercise 4

Refer students to the *Language point* and ask them to decide which sentences in **3** match each rule.

Answers
2 sentences 1 and 3
3 sentence 2
4 sentence 4

Point out that if the *if* structure comes in the second part of the sentence, we do not need a comma between the two parts.

Grammar reference

If students need more information, go to *Grammar reference* on page 125 of the *Student's Book*.

Exercise 5

Students work in pairs to consider ways to improve their city. Remind them that, in each case, they are talking about the result of doing something. Listen out for use of tenses as they talk, and if necessary, prompt and remind them that we do not usually use *will* in the *if* clause.

Possible answers
A What will happen if we improve public transport?
B Some people will stop using their cars, so there will be fewer cars on the roads. If we do that, there'll be less pollution.
Or
A What will happen if we improve public transport?
B It will cost a lot of money, so we'll need to increase ticket prices.
A That won't be popular with the public!
A What will happen if we create more cycle lanes?
B More people will go to work by bike, and it will make the roads safer for cyclists.

Stronger students, or those who finish early, can be asked to come up with their own ideas and results, or even to extend their conversations to add a follow-up result of the suggestion. Other suggestions could include: putting a speed limit on inner-city traffic to e.g. 10 km per hour; banning cars from the city at weekends; creating more green spaces from closed roads, etc.

Further practice

If students need more practice, go to *Practice file 10* on page 125 of the *Student's Book*.

Exercise 6

Students read the instructions about introducing green initiatives and discuss their ideas with a partner. They should then decide which they would choose. Encourage them to have reasons for their answers.

Students could discuss the situation at their school or college.

Give each pair of students a new green initiative, e.g. *Photocopying is only allowed on Fridays.*
We should encourage people to work from home, and have meetings on Skype.
Everyone must use their own mug at work; company mugs are only for visitors.

They should write it at the top of a piece of A4 paper, and then write a full sentence with the result of the initiative. Then pass their paper clockwise round the classroom: each pair now thinks of the next result. Continue rotating the pieces of paper for four or five sentences/results, then pass the papers back to the original pair to read. Which green initiative is the most interesting, or most effective, and why? What are the consequences?

Photocopiable worksheet

Download and photocopy *Unit 10 Language at work worksheet* from the teacher resources in the *Online practice*.

Practically speaking

Exercise 1

Pre-teach *clarification* – making something clearer or easier to understand. Then elicit from the class their ideas about things to say if you don't understand something in a meeting.

Possible answers
Sorry, what did you say?
Could you explain, please?

Exercise 2

▶ **10.3** Ask students to read the sentences, and then listen for the correct answer.

Answer
1 the whole company
2 next year
3 can't
4 part of the day

Exercise 3

▶ **10.3** Students listen again and complete the questions.

Answers
1 Do you mean
2 Sorry, did you say
3 So, are you saying
4 What do you mean by

PRONUNCIATION Ask students to decide which words are important, and are stressed, in each phrase. Encourage them to say each complete question out loud. Model this, or play the listening again, pausing after each question.

Answers
1 Do you <u>mean</u>
2 <u>Sorry</u>, did you <u>say</u>
3 <u>So</u>, are you <u>saying</u>
4 <u>What</u> do you <u>mean</u> by

Exercise 4

Demonstrate the first one with one student first. Students work in AB pairs. Encourage B students to use different phrases for checking clarification. If necessary, first work together with the class to make complete sentences with the cues, e.g. *We need to reduce our energy consumption next year; We must improve the results for recycling*, etc.

PRONUNCIATION In the questions with two alternatives, make sure students use contrastive stress correctly.

1 *Do you mean the <u>twenty</u>-first or the <u>thirty</u>-first of October?*

2 *Are you saying the <u>whole</u> company, or just the <u>factory</u>?*

4 *Sorry, did you say <u>fifteen</u> or <u>fifty</u>?*

Make sure students swap and each have a turn at asking for clarification. Listen out for correct use of phrases.

EXTENSION You could ask stronger students or fast finishers to think of two more ideas, and think of what they would need to clarify, e.g. *We're having a team away day on Thursday.* (clarify *Thursday*, not *Tuesday*)

Business communication

Exercise 1

Let students discuss the question in pairs, then check their ideas with the whole class.

Possible answers
Green policies can save money (by recycling goods or cutting bills) and increase profits / raise awareness of green issues among staff / make the company environmentally friendly to the public / more attractive to job applicants / create a feel-good factor amongst the staff / help cut carbon emissions / reduce air pollution.

Exercise 2

▶ **10.4** Play the listening once for students to compare their list of advantages from **1**. Then play the listening again and ask them to complete the notes. Check answers with the whole class.

Answers
1 energy, profits
2 environment, business
3 employer
4 regulations

Exercise 3

▶ **10.4** Students match the beginnings and ends of the sentences from the presentation, then listen again to check their answers (or read the audio script on page 153).

Answers
1 e 2 g 3 f 4 a 5 b 6 c 7 h 8 d

PRONUNCIATION Ask students to focus on the numbered phrases and to underline the stressed words in each phrase. For example:
I'm here <u>today</u> to <u>tell</u> you about …

I'll <u>come</u> to …

Then ask students to repeat the phrases, paying particular attention to the stressed words. Model the pronunciation yourself, or play the recording and pause at the appropriate places.

Exercise 4

Explain *e-billing*. Explain also that *bill* can be both a noun and a verb – to send someone a bill for something. Check the pronunciation of *secure* /sɪˈkjʊə(r)/, and *security* /sɪˈkjʊərəti/.

Remind students that the notes are only notes, so they need to fill them out with any necessary grammar words, as well as using the expressions in **3** and the *Key expressions*.

Suggested answer
I'm here today to tell you about the switch in our company to e-billing.
First of all, I'll tell you about some of the advantages and disadvantages. *Let's start with* the advantages. For example, customers can view bills at any time of the day or night. In addition, e-billing is faster and cheaper than sending bills by post. Additionally, e-billing helps the environment because it saves on paper and plastic bags used for collecting waste paper. *My next point concerns* the disadvantages: if we switch to e-billing, we'll need special secure software, and not all customers have it. In addition, some customers are still worried about security.
So, to sum up, there are pros and cons, but I believe the disadvantages can be overcome. *That brings me to* the end of my talk. Thank you for listening!

EXTENSION As each student gives their (part of the) presentation, their partner ticks off the phrases they hear. Compare notes at the end to see who used the most phrases!

ALTERNATIVE Have students working as A or B and planning together: Student A could present the topic (subject) and the advantages, and then Student B presents the disadvantages and the conclusion.

Further practice

If students need more practice, go to *Practice file 10* on page 124 of the *Student's Book*.

Exercise 5

Students work in two groups: Group A and Group B. They should work together in groups to help each other and prepare their presentations. When they are ready, pair them up A+B, for them to give their presentations to each other. Listeners should write down the topic of the presentation, and then list some of the advantages and disadvantages they hear: they could then use this information to ask the presenter a question afterwards.

Monitor their presentations and, afterwards, ask them to self-correct if you hear any incorrect use of language: you could write incorrect examples on the board.

PRE-WORK LEARNERS Group A could discuss the advantages and disadvantages of taking holidays without going by air, using the following ideas: ticket prices, distance, destinations, times, tiredness, etc. Group B could discuss using only public transport during the week and for work (not private cars), using the following ideas: cost, time, convenience, carbon emissions, etc.

ONE-TO-ONE The student makes one, two or all of the presentations. You take notes on both content and expressions used, and the student then compares your notes with the list of key expressions. If appropriate, they could prepare this at home for next time.

> ### Photocopiable worksheet
> Download and photocopy *Unit 10 Business communication worksheet* from the teacher resources in the *Online practice*.

Talking point

As a lead-in, write *nudge* on the board and elicit or give the meaning (here – to push somebody gently, in order to get them to change their behaviour; to persuade). Demonstrate the literal meaning (to push somebody gently, especially with your elbow), then explain the meaning here.

Discussion

Exercise 1
Refer students to the text and The Golden Rules of Nudging, and check they understand. Then ask them to read the text and decide which rules the Speed Camera Lottery follows. They could tick off their choices.

> **Answer**
> All of them.

Exercise 2
Students then discuss in pairs any possible disadvantages of the Speed Camera Lottery. Discuss their ideas as a class.

> **Answer**
> It takes time, and someone would need to be paid to do the job.

Exercise 3
Ask students to think of other examples of nudging in everyday life, e.g. getting people to use less electricity, by installing metres in people's homes for each individual electric item; downloading an app which donates money for every 1 km that users walk or run, to motivate people to do more exercise. (The app generates money from advertising.) Discuss ideas as a class.

Exercise 4
Students discuss whether they think nudging works better than rules or punishments. Encourage them to give reasons for their answers.

Task

Exercise 1
Students read the list. Encourage them to come up with at least three ideas for each action. Alternatively, you could allocate one activity to each pair. After five minutes, ask students for a few examples of each initiative. Check they are using the conditional forms correctly.

PRE-WORK LEARNERS Students could talk about the situation where they study.

Exercise 2
In turn, each pair presents their idea to the group. Give them time to prepare, reminding them to use phrases from the *Business communication* section, as well as the language for talking about results from the *Language at work* section.

ONE-TO-ONE You could take two ideas each, and then compare and discuss them. The student could then write up the suggestions for one of the ideas as a mini-presentation, using phrases from the previous section. They could then present it next lesson.

> ### Progress test
> Download and photocopy the *Unit 10 progress test* and *Speaking test* from the teacher resources in the *Online practice*.

11 Entertaining

Unit content

By the end of this unit, students will be able to

- talk about corporate hospitality
- talk about corporate event facilities
- ask about food on a menu
- make invitations and offers.

Context

Corporate entertainment has expanded considerably in recent years. Although the idea of companies 'wining and dining' their clients is well-established, this area of business life has now spawned its own companies who exist simply to provide entertainment and hospitality services for business people. The events fall into two categories: the first type of event are those used to build and reinforce relationships with people outside the company – usually clients, but also service providers, agents, writers, and so on. These tend to be social and sporting events (often involving a lot of eating and drinking): the new Wembley Stadium in London has 18,000 corporate seats (of a total capacity of 90,000, i.e. 20%). The second type of event is provided for the company's own staff, usually to promote team-building and increase motivation. These often involve games like paintballing or problem-solving activities such as murder mystery weekends.

Corporate hospitality is now a massive industry in itself, boosted in recent years in the UK by the 2012 Olympics, the Queen's Diamond Jubilee, the 2014 Commonwealth Games, and the 2016 Rugby World Cup. There is no doubt that the recipients of hospitality enjoy and appreciate it, although whether it makes much difference to clients' decision-making is another matter. In any case, food and drink are an important part of the business person's life.

In this unit, students will start by talking about corporate entertainment. Most contact between business people from different companies will involve food and drink, and the language to discuss it will be immediately useful. Within this context, the language of inviting and accepting or declining an invitation is key, and students are given a number of take-away expressions to help them with it. The *Talking point* at the end of the unit involves discussing the differences between corporate hospitality and bribery.

Starting point

Elicit ideas for 1 from the whole class; students then discuss 2 in pairs.

Working with words

Exercise 1

Students discuss the questions. Encourage them to come up with a list for each answer.

Possible answers

1 to recognize and thank them for their loyalty, to win over their loyalty, to encourage new business
2 the entertainment may be cheaper than offering other discounts or benefits, 'old' and new customers may be more inclined to use their products/services and not those of a competitor

Exercise 2

Students read the text and compare their answers in **1**.

Answers

1 to improve relationships with their customers, suppliers or staff, to give them a good time and be sure of their loyalty in the future
2 Companies consider it good value for money; it can be cheaper than offering a discount.

Check students understand *VIP* /ˌviː aɪ ˈpiː/ (n) – abbreviation for 'Very Important Person', and *to sponsor*.

EXTENSION Ask students if they've ever been involved in any corporate entertainment, either as a company or client. What do, or could, their companies offer for a corporate event? Which clients would they invite?

Exercise 3

Students work in pairs to discuss the questions, based on the information in the text. You could divide the class in two, and ask one group to consider the event organizers and the other to consider ordinary people.

Answers
Event organizers: Advantages: They can sell a large number of tickets at high prices; income is more guaranteed. Disadvantages: they risk being labelled 'elitist'; corporate clients pay more and may expect more.
Ordinary people: Advantages: Higher prices for corporate clients may be used to 'subsidize' ordinary ticket holders. Disadvantages: corporate clients may get the best seats/places; it may be very difficult/impossible to get tickets for major events.

Exercise 4

Students work individually to complete the table, and then compare answers in pairs. Do the first one together. Check answers with the whole class.

Answers

Information	Details
Host company	Banco de Santander.
Guests	Leading VIPs from banking world
Package	Premium seat + champagne + 4-course meal
Venue	Camp Nou Stadium
Event	FC Barcelona vs Real Madrid
Budget	€150,000

PRONUNCIATION Check the pronunciation of these words: *venue* /ˈvenjuː/; *budget* /ˈbʌdʒɪt/; *package* /ˈpækɪdʒ/, and ask students to say them out loud together, focusing on the sounds and word stress.

Exercise 5

▶ 11.1 Students complete the table with information from each speaker, and discuss their answers with a partner. You could draw the table on the board and elicit students' answers.

Answers

	Speaker 1	Speaker 2
Host company	his employer, big electronics company	a big German bank
Guests	its top salespeople	its VIP clients
Venue	five-star hotel in Brazil	*Tristan and Isolde* at La Scala, Milan
Package	all meals and day trips	first class plane ticket, opera tickets, accommodation
Events/ Activities	two-hour convention, a trip to Salvador da Baía, riding quad bikes on a deserted beach	a tour of the opera house, five-course dinner

Check *quad bikes* (n) – four-wheel motorbikes with large tyres; *deserted* (adj) – (of a place) with no people in it.

EXTENSION Ask students which of the two events they would enjoy most as a corporate client and why.

Exercise 6

▶ 11.1 Students match the verbs and nouns, and then listen again to check.

Answers
1 f   2 e   3 d   4 a   5 c (e is also possible)   6 b

EXTRA ACTIVITY
Ask students to list other collocations with these verbs.

Possible answers
hold + a party, a meeting, a reservation, office, an opinion, a conversation
arrange + a meeting, a party, a conference, a loan, an appointment
have + an appointment, an argument, a break, a chance, a conversation, a look, a party
entertain + friends, guests, the audience, the crowd
book + tickets, flights, a restaurant, a hotel, a court (for tennis)
accept + a proposal, an offer, a bribe, the job, money, advice

Exercise 7

Students decide which phrases match the collocations in **6**. Check the answers with the whole class.

Answers
1 have a great time
2 accept an invitation
3 entertain clients
4 arrange a trip
5 book a venue
6 hold an event

Refer students to the *Tip* about the difference between *customer* and *client*. The main difference relates to whether you buy a product or a service. Ask students to give you examples of when they are a customer, and when they are a client. You could prompt by mentioning financial or dental services, or buying products online or on the high street.

Further practice
If students need more practice, go to *Practice file 11* on page 126 of the *Student's Book*.

Exercise 8

Students work in pairs to discuss the questions. Give them a few minutes to work on their own first. Encourage them to use vocabulary from the text and phrases from **6**.

EXTENSION Students swap pairs and tell a new partner about their experience or dream event.

Exercise 9

Students work in small groups to plan a corporate event. Point out that the type of company and the nature of the guests will impact on the size and type of event: motivational events tend to have more games and fewer cultural activities, while events for VIPs are high-status (and budget). Give them five minutes to plan an event using the criteria. Groups report back on their discussions briefly. Listen out for vocabulary and use of verb + noun collocations.

ALTERNATIVE You could give students a fixed budget to work with, and then discuss which group comes up with the best event!

PRE-WORK LEARNERS If students are at school or college, you could suggest they plan an event for visiting teachers or professors from abroad.

ONE-TO-ONE You could suggest the student plans an event at home, and presents their idea next time. Alternatively, brainstorm options together, ask the student to choose the best ones and then present the idea.

Photocopiable worksheet

Download and photocopy *Unit 11 Working with words worksheet* from the teacher resources in the *Online practice*.

Language at work

Exercise 1

Students discuss the question in pairs. Elicit a few ideas from the whole class, asking them to give reasons.

Possible answers
Sporting events are popular with many people, probably more so than, e.g. a night at the opera. Such events are sometimes difficult to get tickets for, and tickets can be expensive, so it can be very special to be invited!

Exercise 2

▶ 11.2 The students will hear two short conversations. Ask them to read the questions, then listen and note the answers.

Answers
Conversation 1: No, the host is still waiting for two guests to arrive. She orders four bottles of mineral water and an orange juice.
Conversation 2: It's 1 p.m. The guest wants to buy some souvenirs for her children.

Exercise 3

▶ 11.2 Students listen again to complete the questions. Check the answers with the whole class.

Answers
1 Are there
2 How many
3 Is there
4 How much
5 Is there

Exercise 4

Students complete the explanations in the *Language point*. Check answers with the whole class. Refer students to the *Tip* about how to describe drinks as countable: ask if they've 'had a coffee' today, or 'an orange juice'. When they go out to a café, what do they usually order?

Answers
1 Countable
2 Uncountable
3 countable, uncountable
4 countable, uncountable
5 countable

Grammar reference

If students need more information, go to *Grammar reference* on page 127 of the *Student's Book*.

Exercise 5

Before doing this exercise, ask students if they have been to Wimbledon to see the tennis, or if they know what it's like. Then ask them to complete the questions. Do the first one together. Check the answers with the whole class.

Answers
1 How much
2 How much
3 How many
4 How many
5 Is there
6 Are there
7 Is there
8 Are there
9 Is there
10 How much

Exercise 6

▶ 11.3 Tell students to listen to the tour guide talking about Wimbledon and note down the answers to the questions in **5**. Then play the listening. If necessary, play it again, pausing after the relevant information. List the numbers 1–10 on the board, elicit the answers from the students, and write them on the board. Find out which pieces of information surprise them, and why.

Answers
1 350,000 cups
2 28,000 bottles
3 125,000 portions of ice cream
4 15,000 bananas
5 Yes, there is.
6 Yes, there's a bank.
7 Yes, with books and videos
8 No, there aren't; only outside the grounds.
9 No, there isn't, but there is help on the website.
10 £27 million

EXTENSION Ask students what events in their own countries would be suitable for corporate hospitality.

Further practice

If students need more practice, go to *Practice File 11* on page 127 of the *Student's Book*.

Exercise 7

Students work in pairs to complete the left column of the table. Remind them to choose a country. Give them five minutes and make sure they both write down the information (this will be needed in **8**). You could encourage them to include something different to attract clients (e.g. a hotel on a boat or underground; each room has a rooftop terrace; breakfast 500 m high; jungle trips, etc.). Monitor and check they complete all the information. For weaker students, demonstrate the activity by discussing as a class first.

ONE-TO-ONE Elicit one or two ideas as examples for the left-hand column for your student, and then, without discussion, each fill in the left-hand column with different information. This is preparation for **8**.

Exercise 8

Re-pair students. They should use the question starters to find out information about their partner's hotel. Give students time to check how to ask the questions. To help make this a phone call, ask students to sit back-to-back. Students listening should note down their partner's information on the right. Listen for correct use of question forms, and countable and uncountable nouns.

Exercise 9

Students return to their original partner to compare information and decide if they want to change anything. Share any changes with the whole group, with reasons: Find out which pair has the most suitable hotel for specializing in corporate hospitality and why. Give feedback on use of accurate language.

> ### Photocopiable worksheet
> Download and photocopy *Unit 11 Language at work worksheet* from the teacher resources in the *Online practice*.

Practically speaking

Exercise 1

Students discuss the questions briefly in pairs. Then discuss some of the answers as a group.

> **Possible answers**
> Read the menu, ask the person you are with, ask the waiter
> Food descriptions can be misleading, there are too many good options to choose from, etc.

Exercise 2

▶ **11.4** Ask students to read the questions and then listen for the information. Check the answers with the group.

> **Answers**
> The woman knows the restaurant.
> **He chooses:** Parma ham, spaghetti carbonara, ice cream
> **She chooses:** tomato and mozzarella salad, lasagne, ice cream

Exercise 3

▶ **11.4** Students match the questions and responses, and listen again to check. Check the answers with the whole group.

> **Answers**
> **1** b **2** d **3** a **4** c

PRONUNCIATION   Ask students to underline the stressed words in the questions and responses. Do the first one together. Point out that we usually stress key information words; however, for emphasis, other words are stressed (e.g. *must* in 1 and *you* in 3). Play the listening again for them to check their ideas. Get the students to repeat the questions and answers, focusing on the stressed words.

1 *What's good here? You must try the Parma ham.*
2 *What are the pizzas like? They're not bad, but I recommend the pasta.*
3 *What are you having? I think I'll have the lasagne.*
4 *What do you recommend? I think you'll like the ice cream.*

Exercise 4

Discuss with the group what they think. You could point out that language in questions is often much more indirect in some cultures to avoid losing face and being embarrassed.

> **Possible answer**
> In many cultures, we ask such questions in order to maintain the right impression, especially when eating with colleagues in similar or higher positions. We don't want to order something that other people might judge negatively.

EXTENSION   Ask your students if they have been in a similar restaurant situation, either asking for or giving advice on a menu. Do they have a favourite restaurant where they like taking friends or colleagues and sharing ideas about the best food there? If so, what makes it special?

Exercise 5

Students work in pairs to have a similar conversation. Make sure one student is the 'expert' who knows the restaurant. Give feedback on their use of phrases. You could put the questions and responses (without the food items) on slips of paper, give a set to each pair, and ask students to turn them over when they use them in their conversation.

EXTENSION   Make the activity into a role-play. Arrange the tables to make a 'restaurant' and appoint a student as the waiter. Ask the waiter to be quite slow, to give the 'diners' time to discuss the menu and make small talk while they're waiting. Use the role-play to recycle functional language: making requests (*Unit 8*) and showing interest (*Unit 3*).

ONE-TO-ONE   Take turns to play the 'expert' at the restaurant.

Business communication

Exercise 1

Ask students to read the three situations and decide how they could make an offer to each person. Accept all answers without correcting, as invitations and offers will be focused on later. Try to elicit that what you offer, and how, depends on who you are talking to, i.e. how formal, informal or neutral.

Exercise 2

▶ **11.5** Students listen and match the conversations to the places.

> **Answers**
> **a** 3 **b** 1 **c** 2 **d** 4

Exercise 3

▶ **11.5** Students listen again to the conversations to complete the invitations and responses. They then match the invitations to the responses. Check the answers with the whole group.

> **Answers**
> **1 e** Would you like to, invitation
> **2 d** Would you like me to, good
> **3 c** Would you like, love
> **4 b** Do you fancy, great
> **5 a** Shall I, asking

Exercise 4

Students decide which conversation is less formal. Elicit their ideas, with reasons. In the more formal expressions, point out that we use *Would you like (to) …?* to make a suggestion for the other person to do something, and *Would you like me to …?* for the person speaking to do something.

> **Answers**
> The speakers know each other well in conversation 4.
> **Inviting:** Do you fancy +-*ing*, Shall I get you …
> **Responding:** That would be great, Thanks for asking, but …

Highlight how intonation helps you sound polite: demonstrate this by contrasting an example invitation with very flat intonation. Model the invitations, or use the listening, pausing after each one. Get students to repeat them with appropriate polite intonation.

Exercise 5

Give the students a few minutes to read the situations. Check they know the following: *Madame Butterfly* is an opera by Puccini; *Picasso* was a 20th-century Spanish painter.

In pairs, students take turns to make appropriate invitations and offers, and either accept or decline.

> **Possible answers**
> 2 Would you like me to make some more copies?
> 3 Do you fancy going to see *Madame Butterfly*?
> 4 Would you like me to drive you to your hotel?
> 5 Shall we / Do you want to stop for lunch?
> 6 Do you want / Would you like me to help you?
> 7 Would you like to go to a Picasso exhibition?

Further practice

If students need more practice, go to *Practice file 11* on page 126 of the *Student's Book*.

Exercise 6

Students could work with a new partner. Refer them to the *Key expressions*. Point out that when we decline an offer, it's usual to give a reason. Encourage students to use different ways to invite their partner and respond appropriately (formal or informal). Monitor their conversations and, afterwards, ask students to try to self-correct if you hear any incorrect use of language: you could write incorrect examples on the board.

Photocopiable worksheet

Download and photocopy *Unit 11 Business communication worksheet* from the teacher resources in the *Online practice*.

Talking point

As a lead-in, write *bribery* on the board and elicit or give its meaning.

Discussion

Exercise 1

Students read the text and, in pairs, think of examples.

> **Possible answers**
> **Bribery:** paying extra to an individual at a company; giving them a gift or special treatment; exchanging special favours between individuals at different companies.
> **Not bribery:** inviting clients to an event (e.g. a concert), taking them for dinner, etc. (Several ideas have been discussed earlier in this unit.)

Exercise 2

Let students discuss this in pairs. Elicit some of their ideas.

Exercise 3

Encourage students to give examples with reasons.

Students could decide on a set of guidelines for a company to ensure their events are 'hospitality' and not 'bribery'.

Task

Exercise 1

Students read the situations and decide if they are bribery or hospitality. Alternatively, allocate one activity to each pair.

Check the following: *to donate*; *to apply for*; *launch* /lɔːntʃ/ *party*; *designer (watch)*.

Ask students for reasons for their opinions. After five minutes, ask them for feedback on the situations.

Check students are aware of the different word stress on these words: *competitive, competition*.

Exercise 2

Students read the expert's view of the situations in **1** and compare it to their own. What do they think of the verdicts?

You could take one or two situations each, and then compare and discuss your views.

Progress test

Download and photocopy *Unit 11 Progress test* and *Speaking test* from the teacher resources in the *Online practice*.

12 Performance

Unit content

By the end of this unit, students will be able to
- talk about performance
- talk about how long and when you have done things
- say complex numbers
- describe performance trends.

Context

Company performance is a key part of business life. Traditional measures of a company's performance include profits, sales and (in the case of a public company) the share price. However, these in themselves are no longer perceived as sufficient. Even the most successful companies need to address the field of corporate responsibility, so a brand leader like Coca-Cola, in its annual report, not only talks about revenues and sales, but also addresses the issue of health and obesity, and talks about the company's involvement with health education programmes. Environmental performance, as we have seen in previous units, is another area where many companies have become acutely aware: for example, on their website, Ford make much of the fact that their plant in Dagenham, UK, won an award for environmental performance and innovation. These factors, rather than being a cost, have become a potential asset.

In this unit, students will discuss and learn key vocabulary to do with evaluating performance. Connected with this is the question of how we describe performance, and, in particular, changes in performance, through statistics and graphs.

The world of business is one where numbers and trends are minutely studied, and some language for describing these, both precisely and approximately, is presented here. The unit ends with a decision-making game which enables students to put into practice the language of the unit.

Starting point

Students read the questions. Elicit ideas for 1 for each category from the whole class, then ask them to discuss 2 in pairs. If students need prompting for 2, you could elicit how a teacher's performance is measured (e.g. through feedback from students, colleagues, exam success).

Possible answers
1 **a company:** profit / output / value (net worth) / reputation / staff turnover
a sportsperson: speed / scores / competition against other competitors / net worth
a government: state of the economy / wealth of the population / crime statistics / contentment of the people / number of people emigrating / prison population / press comment

PRE-WORK LEARNERS Students could answer the questions based on a job they have had or one they would like, or know.

Working with words

Exercise 1

Students rank the different ways of measuring company performance. Stronger students could add to the list.

Exercise 2

You may wish to pre-teach the following: *socially responsible*, *ethnic minorities* and *disabled*.

Students read the text and say which categories in 1 are mentioned.

Answers
how much money it makes, how green it is, who it employs, how safe it is to work there

Exercise 3

Students work in pairs to discuss the questions.

Exercise 4

Students go back to the text and complete the sentences with the words and phrases in bold. Check the answers with the whole group.

Answers
1 workplace diversity
2 socially responsible
3 perform well
4 reputation
5 manage, costs
6 safety record
7 achieve, sales targets
8 environmental performance

Check, or ask students to use their dictionaries to check, the individual sounds and stress in the following words: *achieve* /ə'tʃiːv/; *reputation* /ˌrepjuˈteɪʃn/; *diversity* /daɪˈvɜːsəti/; *safety* /ˈseɪfti/. Encourage them to repeat the words, as a group, with the appropriate sounds and stress.

Exercise 5

Students should be paired with a partner from a different company if possible. They discuss the relative importance of the factors in **4**.

PRE-WORK LEARNERS Students could discuss a company which they know well. An alternative would be for them to research a company out of class, find the answers to the question in **5**, and bring their findings back to class.

Exercise 6

▶ **12.1** Students listen and say which of the factors in **4** is being evaluated. As this activity practises listening for gist, don't pre-teach vocabulary at this point.

Answers
1 workplace diversity
2 safety record
3 performing well
4 environmental performance
5 managing costs

Exercise 7

▶ **12.1** Students read the sentences and try to guess, or remember, the missing words to complete the sentences. Then they listen again to complete the sentences with the adjectives. Check the answers with the whole class. If necessary, check students' understanding of the following: *target; to promote; the darling of sth; incident*. You could point out that the audio says 'We haven't achieved our target of less than 100 accidents per year'. This is a common structure used in spoken English, whereas in written form we would tend to say 'fewer than'.

Answers
1 disappointing
2 encouraged
3 excellent
4 poor
5 satisfactory, average

PRONUNCIATION Check the word stress on the following: *disappointing, encouraging, excellent, satisfactory, average*, and ask students to repeat the words.

Exercise 8

Students match the adjectives in **7** to the definitions. Check the answers with the whole class. Refer students to the *Tip* about adjectives ending in *-ed* and *-ing*, and the examples.

Answers
1 satisfactory
2 average
3 encouraged
4 disappointing
5 excellent
6 poor

EXTRA ACTIVITY
Students draw a line across the page and write the adjectives in **7** along the line from 'good' on the left to 'bad' on the right (answers: *excellent > encouraging > average > satisfactory > disappointing > poor*). What other adjectives could they add? (Possible answer: *outstanding, brilliant, good, fair, adequate, average, bad, terrible, awful.*)

EXTENSION After they have read the *Tip*, ask students if they know any similar pairs of words. (Possible answers: *frightened/frightening, excited/exciting, bored/boring, interested/interesting, tired/tiring, depressed/depressing, amazed/amazing, embarrassed/embarrassing.*) Ask students to write sentences to show their meaning.

Further practice
If students need more practice, go to *Practice file 12* on page 128 of the *Student's Book*.

Exercise 9

Students will need some thinking time before they start speaking. They choose three of the topics and tell their partner about performance using the words in **7**.

Students re-pair to explain their answers. Listen out for, and give feedback on, accurate use of vocabulary from **4** and **7**.

PRE-WORK LEARNERS For the first two topics, students could discuss a company they know well or their place of study.

Photocopiable worksheet
Download and photocopy *Unit 12 Working with words worksheet* from the teacher resources in the *Online practice*.

Language at work

Exercise 1

▶ **12.2** Ask students to read the questions first; then play the recording.

Answers
1 They both work in Dubai.
2 Lionel arrived in 2012; Raul arrived three years ago.

Exercise 2

▶ **12.2** Ask students to listen again and to underline the correct form of the verb. You could ask stronger students to try to underline the correct verb first, before listening. Note that you may need to remind students of the terminology *past simple* and *present perfect*. Check the answers with the whole class.

Answers
1 opened (past simple)
2 had (past simple)
3 has increased (present perfect)
4 've been (present perfect)
5 moved (past simple)

Exercise 3

Students choose the correct option in the *Language point*, and then an example to illustrate it from **2**.

Answers
1 past simple (sentences 1, 2 and 5)
2 present perfect (sentences 3 and 4)
3 since (sentence 3)
4 for (sentences 2, 4)

EXTENSION If the students are having problems with *for/since*, read out the following list of time expressions and ask them to put up their left hand if they would use *for*, and their right if they would use *since*:
2006, ten minutes, the day before yesterday, ten o'clock this morning, an hour, the end of last year, three days, twenty years

Answers
for: ten minutes, an hour, three days, twenty years
since: 2006, the day before yesterday, ten o'clock this morning, the end of last year

NB You could point out that although we can use *for* with both *past simple* and *present perfect*, we usually use *since* with the *present perfect* only.

Grammar reference

If students need more information, go to *Grammar reference* on page 129 of the *Student's Book*.

Exercise 4

Students work in pairs and make sentences using the information in the table. They may need to consult the audio script on page 155 of the *Student's Book*. Note that some students may want to use the present perfect continuous when they see the verbs *working* and *increasing* in the table (e.g. *His business started in 2012 and sales have been increasing since 2014.*). Accept these sentences if they are correct.

Possible answers
Lionel's company has had a sales office in Dubai for X years / since 2012. His business has had more encouraging results since 2006. Lionel arrived in Dubai in 2012. He's lived in Dubai for X years.
Raul has lived in Dubai for three years. Raul's family arrived in Dubai last year. Raul's family has lived in Dubai for a year.

EXTENSION Stronger students, or those who finish early, can be asked to come up with similar sentences about their own situation.

Exercise 5

Start by asking students what they know about Dubai. Students read the information about Dubai and answer the questions. Weaker students could use a dictionary for this.

Possible answers
1 Dubai is trying to build the first non-oil economy in the Gulf.
2 Yes, it has, because it has built a number of popular new tourist and commercial sites, it has opened up its trading and is now able to sell property to non-nationals. Although oil is still important, still generating 2% of GDP, more is being generated from other activities.

Exercise 6

Ask students to read the *Tip* before they do this exercise. As this is the first time they have used the question form of the present perfect, students may need a model on the board:
How long + has/have + subject + past participle?

You could ask a stronger student to read out the example question and give the answer. Do this exercise in two stages: first, forming the questions, and then asking and answering them in pairs.

Answers
2 How long has Dubai invested in services? Since the early 1990s. / For over 25 years.
3 How long has the government allowed non-nationals to buy property? Since 1999. / For over 15 years.
4 When did the Mall of the Emirates open? In 2005.
5 How long has Palm Jumeirah had residents? Since 2006. / For over ten years.
6 How long did it take to build the Burj Khalifa Tower? Six years.
7 When did Dubai win the right to hold Expo 2020? In 2013.

PRONUNCIATION Make sure students pronounce *has/have* with a weak form /həs/ and /həv/; they are used in their strong form /hæs/ and /hæv/ when in an abbreviated answer, e.g. *Yes, it has*, or in a yes/no question: *Have you got …?* Give students examples of both forms and get them to repeat them.

Further practice

If students need more practice, go to *Practice file 12* on page 129 of the *Student's Book*.

Exercise 7

Students work in pairs, and use questions with *How long* and *When* with the appropriate tense to find out things they have in common. Model the conversations first: ask a student: *How long have you been in this room?* The student answers (for example): *Since 11 a.m.* You reply: *Me too! We have one thing in common.* Students read through the list and formulate questions in their heads. Then they ask and answer questions.

To give them more practice with the two tenses, ask students to report back to class using both, e.g. *We have both worked for KME for two years. / We both lived in our last flat for more than five years.*

PRE-WORK LEARNERS Students choose those questions relevant to them, or change the questions about work to relate to their studies. You could also add these ideas to the list: *be in your present class? finish your last school? have your present computer? start learning English?*, etc.

Photocopiable worksheet

Download and photocopy *Unit 12 Language at work worksheet* from the teacher resources in the *Online practice*.

Practically speaking

Exercise 1

▶ **12.3** A fun lead-in could be to ask students if they know the five different ways to say the number 0 in English. (Answer: *zero*, *nought*, '*O*', *nil* (as in football games: 2–0 = two–nil), *love* (in tennis: 15–0 = fifteen–love). Explain that numbers are problematic in English. Students study the numbers for a few minutes and try to say them. (They will probably find this difficult.) Then they listen and check.

Make sure students don't use the plural *four hundreds* or say *one point thirty-nine*. You could tell students that *zero* is always acceptable for the figure 0, especially in American English.

> **Answers**
> one point three nine per cent
> nought point oh three three
> one hundred and two
> seven thousand four hundred and sixty-seven
> nine hundred and six thousand five hundred and seventy

Exercise 2

Students read the sentences, and check their answers together.

> **Answers**
> 1 We use a point before a decimal and a comma to show a thousand.
> 2 We say 'nought' before the decimal and 'oh' after the decimal.
> 3 We use 'and' in British English after 'hundred' (but not in American English).
> 4 We say each number separately after the point.

Exercise 3

▶ **12.4** Students listen and complete the table. Write their answers on the board, and check they say them correctly.

> **Answers**
> Nikkei: + 0.63% = up nought point six three per cent
> FTSE 100: - 58.74 points, = down fifty-eight point seven four points
> DAX: - 0.17% = down nought point one seven per cent
> Dow Jones: - 343.13 points = down three hundred and forty-three point one three points
> Nasdaq: 4,958.47 = four thousand nine hundred and fifty-eight point four seven

Exercise 4

Students use the table to practise saying the figures in **3**. One student speaks; the other listens and corrects.

Make sure students swap and each have a turn at asking for clarification. Listen out for correct use of phrases.

ONE-TO-ONE Do the activity in the same way, but you could introduce a few mistakes (e.g. ways of saying '0'), and ask the student to spot them!

EXTENSION Ask students to find the most recent stock market figures online or in a newspaper, and compare the value, what the change is, and the percentage difference (they may need calculators for this!).

Business communication

Exercise 1

Let students discuss the question in pairs. Students may first want to name the most popular cars, and where they are from. They may also want to discuss what they understand by 'best'! Share some of their ideas with the whole class.

> **Possible answers**
> The following countries should probably be on the list in terms of quantity: India, China, Japan, the United States, South Korea, Germany. Students could try to order them into the top three countries.
> In terms of 'best' cars, the following issues could be taken into consideration: horsepower, acceleration (0–60 km per hour), top speed, safety, fuel efficiency, etc. Other countries to include here could be Britain, Sweden and Italy.

Exercise 2

▶ **12.5** Teach/Elicit the word *trend* and (*horizontal/vertical*) *axis*. Students speculate as to which line represents which country. They then listen and check.

> **Answers**
> 1 China
> 2 USA
> 3 Japan
> 4 Germany

EXTENSION Ask the students if they are surprised by the results, and if so, why.

Exercise 3

▶ **12.5** Students could use a dictionary for this exercise.

> **Answers**
> **Upward:** rise, grow, increase
> **Downward:** decrease, drop, fall, decline
> **No change:** remain stable

Exercise 4

Students ask and answer questions about the graph in **2** in pairs.

Note that for this activity, students will need a few phrases to describe dates, e.g. *in the nineties, in the noughties, since (2000), between (2005) and (2010), from (2010) to (2015), at the start / end of the (noughties)*. You could also teach *will probably* + verb for the future.

Check students know the past simple of these irregular verbs *rise, grow, fall (rose, grew, fell)*.

Exercise 5

Elicit one or two ideas about recent car market trends, and then ask students to discuss this in pairs. If you have a mixed nationality group, put students from the same country together first to plan their answers; then re-pair them with someone from another country. If students have no idea about their local car market, they could research this online for homework, and then present their ideas in the next class.

Listen to what they say, and note down examples of both good and incorrect language, specifically verbs for describing change, and tenses. Afterwards, ask them to self-correct if you hear any incorrect use of language: you could write incorrect examples on the board for group correction.

If you are from the same country as your student, you could suggest they choose a different country to research cars, if they choose to do this task at home.

Exercise 6

Draw students' attention to the prepositions in each sentence. Then ask them to guess which country each sentence refers to. They then write their own sentences. They do this individually, and then get their partner to guess. Monitor, and check specifically on correct use of verbs for describing change and tenses, and prepositions.

Answers
1 USA
2 Japan
3 Germany

EXTENSION Ask students to write down three sentences about the graph in **2**, including the country, but where one piece of information in each sentence is incorrect. They read the sentence to a partner, who has to find out which item is incorrect, and then correct it.

Further practice

If students need more practice, go to *Practice file 12* on page 128 of the Student's Book.

Exercise 7

For this exercise, students may have to find the graph before class or for homework. If this is not possible, and students have no knowledge of their company's/country's performance, ask them to draw a fictional graph (for example, a company's profits 2000–2015) and give it to another student to describe. Students study the *Key expressions* before they start; highlight particularly the phrases for Referring to a chart: these will make their mini-presentation more focused, and audience-orientated. Give feedback on use of tenses, ways of saying numbers, verbs for describing change, and prepositions.

> **EXTRA ACTIVITY**
> Each student brings in a graph they have found (e.g. on the Internet). Shuffle the graphs, and redistribute so that each student has a new graph. Students describe their new graph to the class, or write a description and put it up on the wall next to the graph. Alternatively, when they have written the description, separate the writing from the graph, numbering the graphs, and labelling the descriptions a, b, c, etc. Students read all descriptions and match them to the graphs.

Photocopiable worksheet

Download and photocopy *Unit 12 Business communication worksheet* from the teacher resources in the *Online practice*.

Talking point

Exercise 1

This activity is fairly self-explanatory, so allow students time to read the instructions. Explain that they will win or lose points according to their decisions, and the total number of points they gain will show their company performance, both in terms of sales and profits, but also in social responsibility.

When the students start the activity, make sure that one person in each group is keeping a record of their score (see page 139 for a score for each answer). Check that the students are taking time to discuss each option before moving to the next.

If needed, pre-teach *to promote* (box 3), *injured* (6) /'ɪndʒəd/, *to collapse* (6), *to outsource* (7).

Exercise 2

At the end, each group calculates their final score, and discloses it to the class.

ONE-TO-ONE You could work individually, representing a different company each, and taking individual decisions, and perhaps intentionally make a different choice on some squares. You could challenge the student to give a reason for each decision they make.

Progress test

Download and photocopy *Unit 12 Progress test* and *Speaking test* from the teacher resources in the *Online practice*.

Viewpoint 4

Preview

The topic of this *Viewpoint* is *Green business*. In this *Viewpoint*, students begin by listening to people talking about how environmentally friendly they think their company is. They then watch a video with the Managing Director of the company Edible Oil Direct. Finally, they role-play a situation about biofuel, how it works, and what its benefits are.

Exercise 1

You could start by asking students how environmentally-friendly they are, and what they do to be 'green'. Elicit a few ideas.

Then ask students to read the quiz, and check they understand. Give them two minutes to complete it individually.

Answer
Mostly 'Yes' answers means the company is environmentally-friendly.

PRE-WORK LEARNERS Pre-work students can take the quiz to find out how environmentally-friendly their school or college is.

Exercise 2

Ask students to askeach other questions from the quiz, and then to compare their answers. Elicit any strong differences between them.

Exercise 3

▶ 01 Students watch the interviews and listen for how the four speakers answer the questions.

Ask students if any of the speakers' comments or opinions are similar to their own. Elicit their ideas.

Answers

	Speaker 1	Speaker 2	Speaker 3	Speaker 4
1	Yes (Paper, bottles, coffee, tea bags)	Yes	Yes (lots of different bins)	Yes (Paper, food waste, food packaging)
2	Don't know	Yes	Don't know (probably)	Don't know
3	Yes (Bus, bicycle)	Yes (Cycle-to-work scheme, bicycle loan, showers, bike racks)	Yes (incentives for train and bus tickets and buying bikes)	Yes (Cycle scheme to help pay for bike, subsidized bus passes)
4	Don't know	Don't know	Don't know (probably, especially big things)	Don't know

5	Yes (and use digital versions to save paper)	Yes	Yes (sometimes, depends on quality of product)	Don't know
6	Yes	Yes (a green fairy leaves you a chocolate if you switch everything off)	Yes (most of it, but some lights left on at night time)	Yes (automatically turn off at 6 p.m. and sometimes reward incentives to encourage this)

EXTRA ACTIVITY
You could ask your students to create their own questionnaire and then ask and interview others in the class. The questions could be set out in a similar way to those in **1**, or could be a 'how often' type of quiz. For example: *Do you switch off your computer at the end of the day?: Always, sometimes, rarely, never.*

Exercise 4

Check students understand *edible* (adj): fit or suitable to be eaten; not poisonous.

Students match the words and phrases in bold in sentences 1–8, to their definitions, a–h. Do the first one together.

Answers
1 c **2** a **3** d **4** b **5** e **6** h **7** g **8** f

Exercise 5

▶ 02 Before playing the video, ask students to read the six questions. Each section of the video will answer one of them; the students should put the questions in the right order.

Students check their answers with a partner, then check with the whole class.

Answers
Part 1 d
Part 2 e
Part 3 b
Part 4 a
Part 5 f
Part 6 c

VIDEO SCRIPT

1
What we do here is we retail cooking oils, all types, to the catering trade. We then, when those oils are finished with, we collect those oils, we bring them back here, we refine them and we turn them into a biofuel which is sustainable for all types of applications. And that is the company in a nutshell so to speak.

Basically we are very much into the renewable energy and the company was based on a closed-loop philosophy and that closed loop represents something that has a starting point and has a finishing point, in other words a complete cycle.

2

I wanted to get involved with something that was going to help the environment, which was going to help, like CO_2 emissions, so that was my first stage, and the starting point was selling edible oil which eventually would turn into a biofuel.

3

The fuel that it's going to be, the biodiesel as we call it, is very much sustainable and in fact it lowers the emissions levels, there's hardly any CO_2. It's also a very good lubricating factor for engines and the solvent within that biofuel cleans engines and therefore it really is something for the future or we hope it is, anyway.

4

Well, apart from the, obviously the, the environmental side which is on the emissions and the low CO_2, it's the benefits, it helps the pocket as well. The government have allowed a differential on duty of 20p and therefore that 20p is passed onto the consumer.

5

We've been going now for seven years, just over seven years, and it's been rapid growth. You know, starting from me in a little van delivering oil, we're, we're now approaching a five million turnover per annum. That is going to grow next year. We employ 15 people and we're hoping to introduce another two.

6

The changes are happening all the time with the business, since we first started and I think it's very much the changes are pushing us rather than us pushing the changes. One of the things that we need to do is to try and convince the OEMs, which are the car manufacturers and the truck manufacturers, that biodiesel is a sustainable, clean fuel.

We're also looking to expand the business, the business needs to expand and again, it's not a question of us pushing to expand it, we're being pushed to do that. We've bought a premises which now occupies well over 14,000 square feet, so we're able now to introduce a new biodiesel line which the extra demand from next year for biofuels, from our major customers, and also to portray a better image of our business to the likes of the OEMs. So the future does look bright and it looks green.

Exercise 6

▶ 02 Before playing the video again, ask students to read the text. Then play the video again for students to complete the summary.

Students check their answers with a partner, and then check the answers together.

You may want to deal with any vocabulary students bring up, e.g. *catering trade* (n): the industry which provides food and drinks (for meetings or social events); *lubricating factor* (n): something which helps parts of a machine move smoothly; *solvent* (n): a substance, especially a liquid, that can dissolve another substance; *differential* (n): a difference in the amount, value or size of something; *OEM*: Original Equipment Manufacturer.

ALTERNATIVE Stronger students could be encouraged to try to fill in the gaps before they watch again.

Answers

2 biofuel
3 loop
4 finishing
5 sustainable
6 low
7 20
8 seven
9 five million
10 15
11 green

Exercise 7

Students initially work individually. Divide them into As and Bs. Ask them to read their part and give them a few minutes to plan what they want to say. Monitor and help as needed.

When they are ready, ask students to work in AB pairs. Students A should start. Student B should listen and note down anything extra they want to ask. Then, as appropriate, they should ask Student A their questions. Remind B students that they should reach a decision on whether they want to work with Edible Oil Direct or not!

Monitor and note down any good use of language, especially vocabulary from this *Viewpoint*.

When students have finished, first ask what decisions they reached, and why. You could also elicit from A students what they found easy or difficult in persuading their partners to work together.

ALTERNATIVE If you have a weaker group, you could ask all A students to work together to prepare a presentation, and all B students to work together to prepare questions.

Exercise 8

Let students work individually for five to ten minutes to prepare a short presentation about their own company, or a company they know well. Tell them to make brief notes to help them give their presentation.

PRE-WORK LEARNERS Ask the students to think of a company they know well to give their presentation. They could search for information on the Internet if necessary.

Exercise 9

Put the students into pairs to give their presentations. The student listening to the presentation should take notes and ask follow-up questions at the end.

Further video ideas

You can find a list of suggested ideas for how to use video in the class in the teacher resources in the *Online practice*.

By the end of this unit, students will be able to

- talk about global issues
- make predictions
- link ideas together
- make predictions and forecasts.

Context

The intersection between global issues and business practice is becoming an increasingly important factor in decision making. In the past, the world of business has been accused of 'hiding their head in the sand' when it comes to global issues, but this may not be possible in the future, especially if precious resources start to run out. For example, water running short will have a massive impact on all areas of everyday life, including business. Without water neither small business nor major global industries can function. Water is often taken for granted but if not properly managed, its scarcity will directly affect growth and job creation.

With technological developments happening faster, it may be that technology can provide (part of) the answer in water resource management; this could include, for example, ways of managing efficient water use, providing solutions for water pollution and the collection of rainwater, and methods for re-using waste water.

Some students will also see an ethical side to global issues. For example, on an everyday level, is it right for an office or school to have a water cooler that consumes electricity to cool the water, and plastic for the cups? At a higher level, is it ethical to adopt industrial processes which use a lot of raw materials? Companies that can show they are addressing these concerns may do better with the 'ethical consumer' and hence also improve the bottom line.

In this unit, students will talk about global issues before moving on to look at the language of making predictions, in both a general and a business context. They will also discuss future trends in the workplace. The *Talking point* deals with how consumers can help to make a difference and become more involved in supporting global causes.

Starting point

Elicit ideas for 1 from the whole class, then ask them to discuss 2 in pairs. Elicit some of their answers, with reasons.

Working with words

Exercise 1

Students discuss the sentences. Note that 'consume' (sentence 3) is about general water use, not how much water we drink. Elicit some answers from the group including reasons why, but don't confirm which are correct at this stage.

Exercise 2

Students read the text and compare their ideas from **1**. Elicit whether they were right or not, and why.

Answers
1 True – partly due to the rising demand
2 True – a lot of water is used in production
3 True – (because of 'virtual' water): most people are probably not aware of how much water we consume
4 True
5 False – the problem of water is a global issue

Exercise 3

Students work in pairs to discuss the questions. Prompt them to consider issues at home, as well as at work or college. Discuss some of their answers as a class.

Possible answers
Manufacturing could be at risk if there is a water shortage. Agriculture will be hit directly, which could affect international trade. A lack of clean water, or ways to treat polluted water, could result in disease.
Everyone can become more conscious and work towards being more efficient with water. National and international strategies are necessary, and investment is needed for water infrastructure and management.

PRONUNCIATION Ask students to use their dictionaries to check the individual sounds in the following: *shortage* /ˈʃɔːtɪdʒ/; *threat* /θret/.

EXTENSION Ask students to go online and find other statistics/facts relating to global issues, and then report back to the class.

Exercise 4

Students go back to the text in **2** and match the words in bold to the definitions.

Answers
1 serious threat
2 rising demand
3 economic development
4 global crisis
5 population growth
6 water shortage
7 climate change
8 water supply

PRONUNCIATION Check word stress and ask students to repeat the words: _serious threat, rising demand, economic development, global crisis, population growth, water shortage, climate change, water supply._

Exercise 5

Students work in pairs to discuss natural resources. Students could discuss what they know about how these resources are used, and then what countries use them and what for.

Exercise 6

▶ **13.1** Students listen out for the numbers and what each one refers to. Elicit their answers. Check vocabulary, e.g. _barrel (of oil)_ and _vehicle._

Answers
5%: the possible shortage that would lead to a 400% price increase
400%: an increase in the price of oil
60%: the percentage of total oil used to produce petrol for cars
20: the number of barrels of oil used to produce one vehicle
2.5%: the percentage decrease in petrol consumption needed for oil demand to remain stable
200: the number of years for which we have gas

DICTIONARY SKILLS
Ask students to use their dictionaries to find other words belonging to these families: _analyst, to produce, to consume,_ and to check where the stress is on each word. Encourage students to say each word out loud.
e.g. _to analyse, analyst_ (n. person), _analysis_ (n. object), _analytical_ (adj)

Answers
to pro<u>duce</u>, pro<u>du</u>cer, pro<u>du</u>ction, pro<u>du</u>ced
to con<u>sume</u>, con<u>su</u>mer, con<u>sump</u>tion, con<u>su</u>med

---

Exercise 7

▶ **13.1** Students listen again to complete the sentences.

Answers
1 affect
2 estimates
3 threaten
4 forecast
5 get worse
6 run out of

Exercise 8

Students replace the words in italics with a verb or phrase from **7**.

Answers
1 affects
2 run out of
3 get worse
4 forecast
5 threaten
6 estimates

EXTENSION Ask students to work in pairs, and to choose three of the words above and use each one in a sentence to talk about their own life or close environment, e.g. _They've forecast that unemployment in my country will rise to 9% next year. Climate change threatens many crops._

Refer students to the _Tip_ about using _get_ with comparative adjectives. Ask them to think of one new example each, e.g. _Bread and milk **get more expensive** every year. I think my English is **getting better**!_

Further practice
If students need more practice, go to _Practice file 13_ on page 130 of the _Student's Book_.

Exercise 9

Students work in pairs to discuss the sentences in **8** and answer the questions. Ask them to work alone to think about their answers, and then in pairs try to come up with one solution for each issue. Students could re-pair to explain their answers. Listen out for accurate use of phrases from **4** and **7**.

ALTERNATIVE Ask students to work in pairs or small groups, each one representing a particular country, e.g. China, India, the USA, a country in Africa, a country in Europe, etc. Ask them to think about what the most important issues are, and what action that government could take.

EXTENSION Students could do some online research at home to find out what their country, or a country of their choice, is doing to address the issues in **8**. They could report back to the group next time.

Photocopiable worksheet
Download and photocopy _Unit 13 Working with words worksheet_ from the teacher resources in the _Online practice_.

Language at work

Exercise 1

Write the title of the text on the board and check students understand. To guide their discussion, you could give them the four sub-headings from the text before they start talking. Students discuss the question in pairs and then feed back to the group. They then read the text and decide if the changes in the text are similar to the ones they suggested.

Answers
Competition between businesses will be stronger; managers may need to restructure their companies; retirement at 75; adapting workplace for older workers; more flexible working hours; employees won't need their own desk; more space for meetings and leisure activities.

Exercise 2

Check the following: *to restructure; workforce; flexibility; leisure* /ˈleʒə(r)/ *activities*.

Students choose the correct answer and read the text to check.

Refer students to the *Tip* on short forms of *will*. Practise the pronunciation of *won't* and make sure they can distinguish it from *want*.

> **Answers**
> 1 may
> 2 might not
> 3 will
> 4 won't

Exercise 3

Students complete the explanations in the *Language point* about making predictions, and add an example from **2**.

> **Answers**
> 1 *will*, sentence 3
> 2 *may*, *might*, sentence 1
> 3 *may not*, *might not*, sentence 2
> 4 *will not/won't*, sentence 4

> ### Grammar reference
> If students need more information, go to *Grammar reference* on page 131 of the *Student's Book*.

Exercise 4

Focus students' attention on the table, and ask them to make predictions about the typical workplace in 2030. Encourage them to try to use all the modals listed. NB point out the difference in meaning and word stress between *employer* and *employee*. Elicit one or two suggestions, e.g. *In 2030, many jobs will be part-time. In 2030, management positions might not be easy to find*.

Exercise 5

▶ **13.2** Students listen to a talk about the typical workplace in 2030, and tick what the speaker's predictions are in the table in **4**. Check they know *to exceed* /ɪkˈsiːd/ and *self-managed*.

> **Answers**
> Many jobs will be part-time.
> Management positions may/might not be easy to find.
> More people will work from home.
> Colleagues may/might see each other less often.
> Office buildings will not/won't be used in the same way.
> Employees may/might not want to stay long with the same company.
> Employers will need to offer better working conditions.
> Companies may/might provide leisure facilities.
> Many employees may/might decide to take career breaks.

> ### Further practice
> If students need more practice, go to *Practice File 13* on page 131 of the *Student's Book*.

Exercise 6

Students first make predictions about their own jobs using the ideas given, and the modal verbs in **3**, and then compare in pairs to see if there are any similarities. Give feedback on accurate use of the verbs (*will, may, might* and the negatives).

PRE-WORK LEARNERS Ask students to consider a job they expect to have in two years' time, and how this might change after 10 or 15 years.

> ### Photocopiable worksheet
> Download and photocopy *Unit 13 Language at work worksheet* from the teacher resources in the *Online practice*.

Practically speaking

Exercise 1

Students match the sentence halves. Check their answers together.

> **Answers**
> 1 c   2 a   3 b

Exercise 2

Students decide on the function of each sentence, and check their answers together.

> **Answers**
> 1 so
> 2 and
> 3 but

Exercise 3

Students add the linking words to the categories in **2**.

> **Answers**
> 1 In addition = add more information
> 2 Therefore = show a result
> 3 However = show a contrast

Exercise 4

Students work in pairs to think of ways to complete the predictions using linkers from **2**. Elicit an example first, e.g. *People will work fewer hours, … so they'll receive a lower salary; … and they may do a second job; … but they will work more from home*. Listen to their ideas and check they use the linking words correctly.

EXTENSION Students pair up with another pair of students, and compare their predictions.

> **EXTRA ACTIVITY**
> Students could work in pairs or small groups to make a set of predictions about their own company, or a company they know well, for ten years from now. They could add details, e.g. how many hours people will work, which jobs will be done by computers, how colleagues will communicate without travelling to meet, etc.

Business communication

Exercise 1

Introduce the topic of *teleworking*, and discuss the meaning together. Students work in pairs and discuss the advantages and disadvantages. Elicit some of their ideas.

Possible answers
Teleworking is working at home, but staying in touch with work by phone/email, etc.

	Employee	Company
Advantages	Employees don't waste time commuting; they can be more flexible and comfortable in their work arrangements; they can get a job even if they live somewhere remote.	The company doesn't need to provide so much workspace and car parking; it can increase productivity.
Disadvantages	Employees can feel isolated; it is more difficult to meet clients; it is more difficult to build a 'team'; how can the employer monitor performance?	How can the company monitor performance?

PRE-WORK LEARNERS Students may need a little more prompting and help with ideas if they have no work experience.

Exercise 2

▶ **13.3** Students listen to the discussion of the teleworking scheme, and compare their ideas. If they wrote a list of ideas in **1**, they could tick off the ones they hear.

Answers
Advantages for the employee are that they will feel more motivated, and happier, working from home. Advantages for the company include the fact that he thinks the company will save money in heating, lighting costs, etc., and be able to raise money from renting office space; production usually goes up 10-40%. Disadvantages for the employees are that they won't often see their colleagues. The manager doesn't list any disadvantages for the company.

EXTENSION Ask students if any of them are already involved in teleworking. Are they able to do any of their work from home? What, for them, are the advantages and disadvantages?

Exercise 3

▶ **13.3** Students listen again and complete the sentences.

Answers
1 are, likely
2 hope, will
3 unlikely
4 think, will
5 will definitely
6 probably won't
7 expect
8 Hopefully, will

Check the following: *running costs*; *scheme* /skiːm/; *to rent*; *voluntary* /ˈvɒləntri/.

EXTENSION Draw a cline scale on the board (a long line from left to right). Write *won't* at the far left end, and *will* at the far right end. Write these phrases randomly on the board, and ask students to place them on the cline: *definitely*

will / definitely won't / is likely to / is unlikely to / probably will / probably won't

Possible answer
definitely won't » is unlikely to » probably won't » hopefully won't » hopefully will » is likely to » probably will » definitely will

Point out that *hopefully will/won't* is subjective, so doesn't fit naturally with the phrases above.

Exercise 4

Students work in pairs to rephrase the sentences, using the word in brackets. Ask a student to read out the example. Check the answers together. NB we use *(un)likely to* + verb with the present tense of *be*, but *probably* and *definitely* with *will/won't*. If students need more practice, ask them to write two or three true sentences about themselves e.g. *I'm unlikely to get a new job soon. / I definitely won't work at this company for more than a year.*

Suggested answers
2 We'll definitely save money.
3 Hopefully, I won't work in the evenings.
4 You're likely to find it difficult at first.
5 I probably won't work from home.

Exercise 5

Give students time to read through the ideas. Students work in pairs to role-play the situations, and ask for and make predictions. You could elicit the answer to the example question, and a follow-up question. Remind them to use the target language: *(un-)likely*, *probably* and *definitely*. Give feedback specifically on the target language from this section.

PRE-WORK LEARNERS Ask students to consider the same bullet-point issues relating to an online course, where they learn from home, and perhaps only 'meet' other students online.

Further practice
If students need more practice, go to *Practice file 13* on page 130 of the *Student's Book*.

Exercise 6

Make sure the students understand that the objective of this activity is to practise the language from this section. Ask them to read the *Key expressions*. Give them plenty of time to think about the scenario and to come up with ideas. Ask the class if any students use video-conferencing at the moment, and what its advantages and drawbacks are.

Students pretend to work for the same company, and discuss the proposal from Head Office.

While students are discussing their ideas, make a note of common errors, focusing on the target language of this unit; bring them to the attention of the class at the end: you could write them on the board and ask students to correct them.

ALTERNATIVE You could award points to students for every time they use one of the key expressions, or you could put the expressions on cards for students to turn face down after they use each one.

PRE-WORK LEARNERS Ask students to imagine they work for the same company. They could consider first what equipment they have, or need, what business trips they currently make, and what training is currently in place. Then ask them to think about what effects the cut-backs will have.

Photocopiable worksheet
Download and photocopy *Unit 13 Business communication worksheet* from the teacher resources in the *Online practice*.

Talking point

Write *cause marketing* on the board and try to elicit from the students what it means. Then ask them to read the first paragraph. Elicit any ideas or examples of cause marketing.

Students then read the three examples. Check they understand the following: *slogan*; *to donate*; *stereotype*; *initiative*.

Discussion

Exercise 1

Students read the question and discuss their answers.

> **Possible answers**
> (a) good PR: it makes people think the company has good corporate social responsibility (CSR); the company is advertised through activities consumers carry out; they may attract and retain customers and employees, and attract new investors and customers, as people may prefer doing business with companies who support a good cause.
> (b) it saves them having to do some fundraising and raises their profile; the activities help raise awareness of important causes; they help people contribute indirectly through taking part in or buying something.

Exercise 2

You could ask pairs or groups of students to choose one of the companies and think about why the companies chose these causes. Share their ideas with the group.

> **Possible answers**
> TOMS: This campaign highlights the issue of the haves and have-nots: for every item bought, the buyer knows they're helping one other person in need.
> Unilever: This campaign suggests, ironically, that cosmetics do not necessarily make people beautiful; however, all consumers who buy such products are interested in caring for their looks, health and/or well-being.
> General Mills: Food is in everyone's house, so these products target a huge range of users, many of who will be interested in educational resources.

Exercise 3

Students work in pairs to find similarities and differences between the companies. Share ideas as a group.

> **Answers**
> In each case, the company is raising awareness of a social issue; in the first and third examples, the companies are actively giving something to someone else (a similar item, or one related in the first; 10 cents per box top in the second).

Exercise 4

Students discuss their preferences. Discuss reasons as a group.

Task

Exercise 1

Students work in pairs or small groups to plan a cause marketing campaign, based on the ideas given. Give them six or seven minutes to do this, and prompt with help if needed.

PRE-WORK LEARNERS Students could choose a company they know, and pretend they work for it.

ONE-TO-ONE Work together with the student on planning a cause marketing campaign, or, alternatively, ask the student to plan one at home, and then evaluate it together next time.

Exercise 2

Before students present their ideas, discuss how to evaluate the campaigns, i.e. what results do you want to achieve a) for the for-profit company, b) for the non-profit organization, c) for the beneficiaries, etc.

Each pair or group should choose a spokesperson to present their ideas to the class. Students then discuss which one(s) is/are likely to be the most successful and why. You could base this on the results each group aimed to achieve.

Make a note of any incorrect language; put these on the board for whole-class correction.

EXTENSION Ask students to search online for other examples of cause marketing and report back to the class next time.

Progress test
Download and photocopy *Unit 13 Progress test* and *Speaking test* from the teacher resources in the *Online practice*.

14 Time

Unit content

By the end of this unit, students will be able to

- talk about time management
- speculate and discuss consequences using the second conditional
- talk about deadlines
- negotiate conditions.

Context

Time management is an important issue in current business thinking, and large numbers of experts, companies and websites have sprung up to help us with it. Some of these undoubtedly provide useful advice, especially on how to deal with modern technology, which, although it supposedly makes our lives easier and quicker, often clogs them up with emails and texts. From the students' point of view, especially if they are pre-work learners, time management has an extra significance because it is useful for their study as well as their work.

There is also a cultural element. Some cultures, for example, approve of somebody who works long hours, whilst others will see them as inefficient and probably a time-waster. Also, traditionally (and perhaps stereotypically), we tend to divide cultures into those where time and punctuality are important and those where people are more relaxed about it. This divide has become more significant as business becomes global, and we can end up working with colleagues of any background.

The second area in this unit is negotiation. Different cultures negotiate differently, and it is not the case that the Western norm of working towards a compromise is necessarily accepted by all.

Both these topics should provide a good starting point for intercultural exchange if you have a suitable class. And in both areas, we could ask the question: does an individual person's attitude derive mainly from their culture, or simply from their own personality? This unit helps the students to explore these questions. They will also learn about negotiating, and practise what they have learnt throughout the unit in the *Talking point* on work–life balance.

Starting point

Elicit ideas for 1 from the whole class, with reasons, then ask them to discuss 2 and 3 in pairs. Elicit some of their answers, encouraging them to give examples (as long as this doesn't embarrass anyone).

Remind students that we use *always*, *sometimes* and *never* before the main verb, but after the verb *be*, e.g. 'I'm *sometimes* late for meetings'; 'I *never* finish work on time'.

PRE-WORK LEARNERS Replace the sentences in 2 with the following

- I organize my study time well.
- I have a lot of interruptions while I'm studying. OR I'm easily distracted when I study or work.
- When I have assignments to do, I hand them in on time.

Working with words

Exercise 1

Write *multitasking* on the board and elicit the meaning. Ask *Do you have to multitask in your job/studies?* Then ask students to answer and then discuss the questions in pairs.

Exercise 2

Students read the text and find the answers to the questions in **1**. Check *keyboard*. Note that in British English we say *schedule* /'ʃedʒuːl/, but in American English /'skedʒuːl/.

Answers
1 b 2 b 3 a

Exercise 3

Students discuss their own habits and situations, and compare them in pairs. Discuss some of their ideas with the whole group.

Exercise 4

Students choose the correct words to complete the sentences.

Answers
1 waste
2 plan your schedule
3 allow
4 enough, deadlines

EXTENSION If students have trouble differentiating between *save time* and *spend time*, give these examples: *save time* is the opposite of *waste time*, e.g. 'We'll take a taxi to save time. It's faster than the bus.' *Spend time* is using time for a specific purpose, e.g. 'I spent an hour doing my homework.' Ask students to write a sentence to illustrate each meaning.

Exercise 5

Students work in pairs to make sentences using the phrases. Elicit one or two first to help. When they have finished, elicit some examples from the group.

Possible answers

When you don't meet deadlines, your customers aren't happy.
Our meetings never finish on time.
You save time when you take a plane instead of a train.
I spend time watching TV every evening.

EXTENSION Find out what different ways students use to meet deadlines and save time. They could share these with the group!

Exercise 6

Students could work with a new partner to discuss time management. Encourage them to use the ideas listed, perhaps deciding on which issues cause the most problems. Elicit an example first, e.g. *I often have a lot of phone interruptions. This means that I can't always meet deadlines.*

PRE-WORK LEARNERS Ask students to think about their own time management, tasks and deadlines, and interruptions, e.g. doing assignments, social media (e.g. Facebook), family commitments, etc.

Exercise 7

▶ 14.1 Students listen and match the speakers to the situations in **6**. Ask students if any of their difficulties with time management are similar to those they heard. Check students know *agenda* – a list of items to be discussed at a meeting.

Answers
Speaker 1: meetings
Speaker 2: administrative tasks
Speaker 3: difficult deadlines
Speaker 4: phone interruptions

Exercise 8

▶ 14.1 Before playing the listening, ask students to try to remember what words are missing. Then play the recording again for them to complete and check the sentences. Refer students to the *Tip* about *in time* and *on time*, highlighting the different focus. Ask them to write a sentence for each phrase.

Answers
1 late
2 save
3 run out
4 take, allow
5 last
6 ahead
7 in
8 waste, slows

Exercise 9

Students work in pairs to write the phrases from **4** and **8** under the correct headings.

Answers
Good: plan your schedule, allow time, save time, enough time, arrive ahead of time, in time, on time, meet deadlines
Bad: waste time, run out of time, leave until the last minute, slow you down

Further practice

If students need more practice, go to *Practice file 14* on page 132 of the *Student's Book*.

Exercise 10

Give students time to think how they use their own time, and how others use their time. They then compare in pairs and discuss how to manage their time better. Listen out for good use of phrases from **4** and **8**. Share the best suggestions with the group. Give feedback on good use of phrases; any which need correcting could be corrected together as a group.

Photocopiable worksheet

Download and photocopy *Unit 14 Working with words worksheet* from the teacher resources in the *Online practice*.

Language at work

Exercise 1

Students read the questions. Discuss some of their answers as a group, with reasons, e.g. *What made their time abroad enjoyable? Would they like to work abroad and why / why not?*

PRE-WORK LEARNERS Discuss the same questions but about studying. i.e. *Have you ever studied abroad?*

Exercise 2

▶ 14.2 Students read the two questions, and then listen and answer the questions.

Answers
1 Yes
2 Only for a short time

Exercise 3

▶ 14.2 Before playing the listening again, ask students to try to underline the correct option. Then play the recording. Check the answers together. Point out that in sentence 3, both *might* and *would* are grammatically possible (see *Tip* below).

Answers
1 I'd, lived
2 would, offered
3 was, might
4 wanted, wouldn't

Exercise 4

Students read the sentences in **3** again, and choose the correct words to complete the explanations in the *Language point*. Refer students to the *Tip* on *might* and *could*. Ask students to write a sentence to illustrate the use of each word.

Answers
1 imaginary, future
2 past, infinitive
3 can

Grammar reference

If students need more information, go to *Grammar reference* on page 133 of the *Student's Book*.

Exercise 5

Students complete the questions with the correct form of the verbs. Check the answers together. Point out that we don't use *would* in the 'if' clause.

Exercise 6

Students work in pairs to ask and answer the questions in **5**. Encourage the use of *might* where appropriate. Listen out for accurate use of second conditional sentences in their answers. Give feedback on good examples; you could write any mistakes you hear on the board and ask students to correct them.

Further practice

If students need more practice, go to *Practice File 14* on page 133 of the *Student's Book*.

Exercise 7

As a lead-in, ask students about attitudes to time and punctuality in their country. Write *clock time* and *event time* on the board; ask them what they think the phrases mean. Students read the text and answer the questions in pairs. When discussing the questions, be ready for some lively responses: some students may object to cultural stereotypes.

Exercise 8

Students work in pairs. Student A turns to page 139, and B to page 142. Ask them to read the task examples carefully: make sure they understand that they need to make questions using the second conditional from the information given.

Check they understand *quotation*, *irritable* and *checkout*.

Students answer the questions first for themselves, and then for their partner, noting down both sets of answers. They then look at page 140 to add up their score, and compare together. Leave time to discuss results with the group. Ask how accurate they think the quiz is for defining their use of time.

EXTENSION Stronger students could write an extra quiz question, with three answer options. They could then ask the group to answer this.

Photocopiable worksheet

Download and photocopy *Unit 14 Language at work worksheet* from the teacher resources in the *Online practice*.

Practically speaking

Exercise 1

▶ 14.3 As a lead-in, you could ask students if they are flexible about time and deadlines. Elicit some examples. Students listen to the two conversations and answer the question.

Exercise 2

▶ 14.3 Before listening, ask if students can remember the phrases they heard. Then play the recording again for them to match 1–7 to a–g. Check the answers together.

PRONUNCIATION Point out that in these phrases, we usually link sounds, e.g. *as soon as possible* /əzsuːnəz'pɒsəbl/. Point out also which word we stress, i.e.
as soon as <u>possible</u>; when you have <u>time</u>, right <u>away</u>, before the <u>end</u> of next <u>week</u>.

Exercise 3

Students decide which two phrases do not give a deadline, and then order the others, from the most to the least urgent. Remind them to work from today as Wednesday. You could help, as follows: *by* means 'on or before' and is used with specific times or days/dates; *on* is used with a day or date; *within* means inside a period of time.

Exercise 4

Students work in pairs, taking turns to ask for things in sentences 1–6, using the words in brackets. Their partner, B, responds using a different time expression. Model first, if necessary. Before starting, check they can form the correct phrase with the word in brackets. For stronger students, suggest that they use different ways to start each request, e.g. *Could you / Can you / I'd like to / I need to* …, etc.

Give feedback on correct use of time expressions, as well as conditional sentences, if students use them.

PRE-WORK LEARNERS Students can use the prompts in **4**, or make up their own ideas for deadlines, e.g. assignment, essay, tutorial, seminar, etc.

Ask students to look up the following verbs to find out the verb patterns (including prepositions). The answer may be in the grammar information in the dictionary, or in the examples. Do the first one together.

1 waste time
2 succeed
3 plan (v)
4 propose
5 offer (v)
6 agree

Answers
1 + -ing / + on + -ing
2 + in + -ing
3 + to + verb / + on + -ing
4 + to + verb / + -ing
5 + to + verb
6 + to + verb / + that + subject + should/would, etc.

Then ask them to choose three verbs and use them to write three sentences about their own situation, e.g. I succeeded _in passing_ my exam! / I plan _to study / on studying_ in the UK.

Business communication

Exercise 1

Introduce the topic of sales and suppliers. Students read the question. Discuss some of their answers as a group.

Possible answers
Deliveries are late; suppliers run out of stock; the company has technical problems, etc.

Students may need a little more prompting to think about all the things involved in supplying goods, e.g. staff, materials, transport, etc., before coming up with ideas.

Exercise 2

▶ 14.4 Check the following: _machine, tool, manufacturer_. Students read the instructions, speculate about the problem (and solutions), and then listen and complete the information. Point out the use of _basically_ to introduce an explanation.

Answers
Problem: a lorry drivers' strike. Luca won't be able to deliver the order on time.
First solution: sending the goods by train
Disadvantage: the order won't arrive in time for production.
Second solution: train to the border, where a lorry from Hans-Peter's company will pick it up.
Who will pay: Luca's company, the supplier

Exercise 3

▶ 14.4 Before playing the listening, ask students to try to match the sentences halves. Then they listen again and check their answers.

Answers
1 c 2 d 3 i 4 a 5 g 6 h 7 j 8 e 9 b 10 f

Ask students to listen to the conversation again and mark the sentence stresses, e.g. _We have an issue with delivery_.

Answers
1 We have an issue with delivery.
2 Basically, we've got a lorry drivers' strike here.
3 Would it be OK if we sent them by train?
4 Yes, that might be possible.
5 What if we transported them by train to the border?
6 Could you send a lorry to pick them up?
7 I think we could do that.
8 That would allow us to get the parts to the factory in time.
9 Would you agree to pay the extra cost?
10 Sorry, that wouldn't be acceptable.

Exercise 4

Students decide which phrases in **3** have which function. Do the first one as a whole class. Check the answers together.

Answers
1 1, 2
2 3, 5
3 8
4 6, 9
5 4, 7
6 10

Give the class one word from a sentence in **2** as a prompt to elicit the sentences. Students must produce the sentences using the prompt word. Then they do the same in pairs. You could also ask students to add an appropriate gesture each time they use one of the phrases, e.g. to reject a solution, they shake their head; to agree, they nod; etc. NB gestures can be culturally sensitive, so this will need careful introduction.

Exercise 5

Before doing this exercise, students will need practice of the phrases in **3**. Refer them also to the _Key expressions_.

Tell students they will be discussing the supply of computer processors. They study the situation in **5**, and think of ways to use the sentences from **3** in the new context. Weaker students could write their ideas down first; alternatively, divide the class into two: all student As work together, and Bs together: they plan what alternatives to offer or suggest.

You could elicit or demonstrate the conversation on the board first, without giving all the answers, e.g.

A We have an issue with delivery. Basically, ... [explains problem], etc.

B Yes, that might ..., etc.

Students work in pairs to negotiate according to the instructions.

To give further practice, and help increase fluency, ask students to do the activity again, swapping partners, and roles. Give feedback on the phrases for negotiating, appropriate sentence stress and use of second conditionals.

Further practice

If students need more practice, go to _Practice file 14_ on page 132 of the _Student's Book_.

Exercise 6

Refer students to the *Key expressions* and check stress and intonation again. Then ask the students to work in AB pairs and to read the relevant information. Check vocabulary and that they understand the situation. Stress that the aim of the negotiation is to come to an agreement! Students then negotiate using the expressions.

With a weaker group, ask pairs of A students to work together to plan what they want to say, and B students to work in pairs to anticipate what A will ask and to think about how to respond.

When giving feedback, focus first on the outcome of their negotiation; students are likely to be interested in how other pairs negotiated, and who was the 'best' negotiator. Then give feedback on their use of the target language.

Photocopiable worksheet

Download and photocopy *Unit 14 Business communication worksheet* from the teacher resources in the *Online practice*.

Talking point

Write *work–life balance* on the board. Elicit from the students what they understand by it and what their own work–life balance is like.

Then focus students on the infographic, and elicit briefly one or two comments and opinions on what they understand.

Check students understand *HR* and *to sacrifice*.

PRE-WORK LEARNERS If you have students who are at school or college, ask them to think about how they manage their study and leisure time.

Discussion

Exercise 1

Students discuss in pairs what they can learn about working life in America from the statistics. Elicit some ideas from the group.

Possible answers
Working life in America is taking up far more of people's time than it used to. Family life is suffering, as regular sit-down meals are now more infrequent. Social lives also suffer, as work becomes more important.

Exercise 2

Students compare this with the situation in their own country and try to imagine what the statistics would be.

Exercise 3

Elicit one reason from the group for why we are busier now, and then ask each pair to come up with one more reason.

Possible answers
Competition for jobs is probably much tougher than it used to be, and there is rarely nowadays such a thing as a 'job for life'; this means that many people are willing to work harder in order to try not to lose their job. In addition, many jobs are now done by computer, or done more quickly online, so more jobs are under threat. To survive we need to work more, and work harder, and as a result most people are busier.

Task

Exercise 1

Students work in pairs or small groups to read the questions, and come up with answers to improve the work–life balance of employees. Remind them to add any extra ideas of their own to the list. Monitor and make a note of good examples of language use, as well as any that need correcting.

PRE-WORK LEARNERS Students could choose a company they know, or an ideal company, and answer the questions based on this.

Exercise 2

Each pair or group chooses a spokesperson to present their ideas to the class. You could then discuss which ideas would be most successful in ensuring a suitable work–life balance.

Give feedback on their ideas, as well as on accurate language use, and any which needs correcting.

EXTENSION Stronger students could consider the effect of the measures they introduce on the company: they could consider issues such as costs, staff needed to run children's activities, office space and job-sharing, etc.

Progress test

Download and photocopy *Unit 14 Progress test* and *Speaking test* from the teacher resources in the *Online practice*.

Unit content

By the end of this unit, students will be able to

- talk about personal development and training
- give advice using modal verbs
- give and respond to positive feedback
- make and respond to suggestions.

Context

Improvement – in the form of personal development and *Training* – is a key issue in business today. Since the students will, by definition, be undertaking a training course of some kind, it should be an area of relevance to them. Staff changes and turnover are more frequent than in the past, and one path to finding better jobs and gaining promotion is through gaining extra skills. The companies that offer this are more likely to retain staff. Some companies may complain that they train the staff, who then leave. But the alternative is *not* training them – and then they will leave. Or, worse, they'll stay!

Professional development (i.e. the development of technical skills to do with the job) has always been seen as the responsibility of the employer, but increasingly personal development is, too. This is linked with the need to motivate staff through setting and achieving goals, appraisals to check progress, and giving constructive feedback on performance. Many managers are not trained to do these tasks, which can cause problems.

These issues are explored in the unit, which also gives the students the language and tools to give advice, suggest solutions, and reassure colleagues in difficult situations. The *Talking point* at the end of the unit allows students to review some of the important grammatical points from the course.

Starting point

Briefly elicit one or two pieces of information for question 1 from the class, and then ask students to discuss both questions in detail with a partner. If students need prompting, you could use yourself in the role of a teacher to give one or two examples.

Discuss answers as a group.

PRE-WORK LEARNERS Encourage students to think about a job they would like and what they know about training opportunities.

Working with words

Exercise 1

Write *coach* on the board and elicit what students understand by it. They should be familiar with a sports coach, who trains their team and encourages them. Elicit a few ideas from the group on what they think a business coach does.

Exercise 2

Students read the text and compare with their answers from **1**. Check students understand *impressive*.

Suggested answer

A business coach helps managers improve their performance. Specifically, they help set goals and achieve objectives. They can improve an individual's promotion prospects, and help motivate them. A coach also gives feedback and helps identify training to further develop skills.

Exercise 3

Students discuss the questions in pairs. Discuss some of their ideas with the whole group.

Exercise 4

Students match the words and phrases in bold in the text in **2** to definitions 1–8.

Answers

1 take a step back
2 motivate
3 develop your skills
4 improve your performance
5 set goals
6 achieve your objectives
7 improve your promotion prospects
8 give feedback

PRONUNCIATION Ask the students to underline the main stress in each phrase.

Exercise 5

Students complete the sentences with words and phrases from **4**. Then they ask and answer the questions. Focus on the *Tip* and the difference between goals and objectives. Ask each student to think of an example of their own for each word.

PRE-WORK LEARNERS Change the questions to:

1 What things _____ you to study hard?

2 At the start of this course/year, did you _____ any _____? What are you doing to try and _____ them?

3 How often does your teacher _____ you _____ on your performance?

4 Do you think training would be the best way to _____ a person's _____ _____? What other ways are there to move up in the company?

5 When is the best time for somebody to _____ a _____ _____ from their job?

6 What new _____ would you like to _____ in your personal or academic life?

7 Have you done any training courses recently to _____ your _____ at school or college? How have these courses helped you?

EXTENSION Elicit from the group anything particularly interesting they found out about each other.

Exercise 6

Students match the training course titles to their descriptions. Check their answers with the whole group.

EXTENSION Ask your students if they have done any courses such as those listed and, if so, how useful they were.

Further practice

If students need more practice, go to *Practice file 15* on page 134 of the *Student's Book*.

Exercise 7

▶ **15.1** You could introduce this listening by asking in what situations managers meet employees. Ask for some examples from their own businesses. How many of the meetings are accidental and how many planned?

Students read the situations, and listen to match the extracts to the situations. Check they understand *annual appraisal*.

Exercise 8

▶ **15.1** Students listen again and identify what Scott is doing wrong. Then they look back at the list of courses in **6** and decide which courses he should take and why. You might want to point out that the language used is very direct, e.g. conversation 1, 'you never told me that'. Advise students that this language may not be appropriate in a business context.

Exercise 9

Students work in pairs. They should read the questions and share their answers about which courses they think would be good for them, and why. They could write their reasons down. Elicit some of their answers and discuss as a whole group. Give feedback on correct use and pronunciation of phrases from **4**.

PRE-WORK LEARNERS Brainstorm a list of short courses the students have been on, or heard about and considered, and write these on the board. Then ask them to discuss the questions in pairs.

ALTERNATIVE If your students haven't done, or don't plan to do any training courses, ask them to assess the courses in **6** and say which could be useful for them in their studies or at work.

Photocopiable worksheet

Download and photocopy *Unit 15 Working with words worksheet* from the teacher resources in the *Online practice*.

Language at work

Exercise 1

If your class has a lot of work experience, you could ask them to exchange experiences of appraisals and decide what makes a good or poor one.

Students read the advice as if the gaps are not there, and say if they agree or not. (Note that some of the points are actually the opposite of what is advised in **2**.) Briefly discuss some of their answers as a class.

Exercise 2

▶ **15.2** Students listen and compare the speaker's advice with their own opinions from **1**. Check the answers with the class.

Answers
1 No
2 No
3 Yes, especially if they are shy
4 Yes
5 Yes
6 Yes

Exercise 3

▶ **15.2** Students listen again and complete the advice in **1** with the correct modal verb. Check the answers with the class. If students ask you for the meanings of the verbs at this point, tell them you will study this in the next activity.

Answers
1 shouldn't
2 mustn't
3 could
4 should
5 should
6 must

PRONUNCIATION Make sure students don't pronounce the middle /t/ in *mustn't*.

Exercise 4

Students read and complete the sentences in the *Language point* using a modal verb from **3**. Refer students to the *Tip* box on *have to* and *must*. Ask students to write their own two sentences, one for an 'outside' request, and one for something they personally believe is important. Discuss some of their examples as a group.

Point out that the question form for both verbs is usually with *have to*, e.g. *Do you have to wear a uniform?*

Answers
1 must
2 should
3 could
4 shouldn't
5 mustn't

EXTENSION You could extend the *Tip* to talking about the difference between *don't have to* and *mustn't*, where there is a clear distinction in meaning. *You don't have to do something* means it is not necessary but you can if you want. *You mustn't do something* means it is not allowed or strongly inadvisable.

Grammar reference

If students need more information, go to *Grammar reference* on page 135 of the *Student's Book*.

Exercise 5

Note that the answers to this exercise are highly subjective and could provoke interesting discussion. Give the students

time to read through the advice, and monitor for vocabulary problems.

Students read the sentences and decide what they think of the advice. Don't let them discuss the ideas yet, as that is the focus of **6**.

Exercise 6

Students discuss the ideas in **5** using modal verbs from **3**. Focus on correct use of modals. Make sure they contract the negatives and pronounce *mustn't* correctly. Use their reasons to check they have understood the concept of each modal.

Exercise 7

Students read the profiles. Ask students if they know anybody in a similar situation. Students discuss the advice they would give each person in pairs. Make sure they use the modal verbs from **3** when they are talking about advice.

Exercise 8

▶ **15.3** Students listen to the experts and compare their answers in **7**.

Answers
Marek:
Should try to take some holiday and spend time with his family
Needs to work on his management skills
Should ask for training in time management and managing people
Could hire a personal coach
Must talk to his team
Should set clear goals for his team
Klaudia:
Should talk to her boss
She could ask him how to improve her promotion prospects
She could speak to the CEO, but she shouldn't do this immediately
She could say she might leave

Further practice

If students need more practice, go to *Practice file 15* on page 135 of the *Student's Book*.

Exercise 9

Give students time to read the list, choose two topics and come up with some advice. Students then ask their partners for advice on how to do these things. Tell them they should formulate the problem properly using the prompts e.g. *I don't feel motivated in my current job, and I need some advice on how to increase my motivation.* The other student listens and gives advice using the modal verbs. Encourage use of all five verbs from **3**.

EXTENSION If you have students from different places of work, you could ask them to talk about a colleague they know and ask for advice on how they can do their job better. If students are from the same company, this is probably not advisable!

Photocopiable worksheet

Download and photocopy *Unit 15 Language at work worksheet* from the teacher resources in the *Online practice*.

Practically speaking

Exercise 1

Students read the situations, and decide what they could say as a response. Elicit a possible response for the first one, and then ask students to work in pairs and come up with other alternatives.

Possible answers

a Thank you! / That was really interesting / I really enjoyed your talk.

b Thank you. It's mostly fine, but it would be good if you … / it still needs a bit of work on it.

c This is excellent. / Thank you very much. / I'm really pleased with what you've done.

Exercise 2

▶ 15.4 Students listen and match each conversation with one of the situations in **1**.

Answers
1 a **2** c **3** b

EXTENSION Ask students if they have been in any of these situations recently, giving feedback on something. What was it, and what did they say?

PRE-WORK LEARNERS If students are at college, ask them if they have recently been given feedback on any of their coursework. What did their tutor say? Was it appropriate? Why/Why not?

Exercise 3

▶ 15.4 Students listen again and complete the phrases in A for giving feedback, and in B for responding. Encourage students to practise the conversations with a partner.

Check students understand *to hire* and *sales rep* (representative). You could point out that using a person's name when giving feedback makes it much more personal and appropriate.

Answers
A: enjoyed, helpful, job, done, had, track, just
B: liked, hear, bad

PRONUNCIATION Point out that we use intonation to make feedback sound positive and encouraging. If necessary, play the listening again and ask students to mark which words and phrases are said at a higher pitch (using a wider intonation), and which sound more friendly. Encourage them to repeat the phrases, stopping and starting the listening at appropriate times.

Exercise 4

Students work in pairs, taking turns to give and respond to feedback in situations 1–4.

Give feedback on good use of phrases and appropriate intonation. You could elicit a suitable response to your feedback from the students!

Business communication

Exercise 1

Ask students what ideas they have for motivating employees or college students, e.g. a suggestions box. Elicit other ideas from the group. Students read the three ideas for motivating employees. Ask them which is best for them. Elicit one or two ideas from the group. Then ask students to discuss them in pairs. Elicit any other ideas which help motivate them.

PRE-WORK LEARNERS Ask students who are studying at college to think of what motivates them to study and do course work. Answers could include, e.g. the prospects of getting a good/better job; getting good grades and results; learning about new topics and areas of work, etc.

Exercise 2

▶ 15.5 Pre-teach *defective* – having a fault or faults; not perfect or complete. Students listen to the conversation about team motivation and put the points in **1** in order.

Answers
a 2 **b** 3 **c** 1

Exercise 3

▶ 15.5 Before playing the recording, ask students to try and match the suggestions and responses. Then students listen again to complete the sentences, and check their answers.

Answers
1 c **2** d **3** a **4** f **5** e **6** b

PRONUNCIATION Ask students to decide which word (or parts of words) in both the suggestions and the responses is stressed, e.g.

Why don't we start with moti<u>va</u>tion? <u>Good</u> <u>idea</u>.
You could explain the <u>value</u> of their <u>work</u>. <u>Yes, that</u> might work.
You should <u>always</u> give <u>feed</u>back. <u>Well</u>, I'm <u>not</u> <u>sure</u> about that.
I <u>suggest</u> you send <u>each</u> person an <u>email</u>. <u>Yes, that's</u> not a bad <u>idea</u>.
<u>What</u> about <u>introducing</u> a <u>team</u> project? I <u>don't</u> think that would <u>work</u>.
Shall we <u>talk</u> about how to <u>put</u> them into <u>prac</u>tice? <u>Yes</u>. <u>Let's</u> do that.

Exercise 4

Students decide which group the responses belong to. Check the answers. NB *That's not a bad idea* is actually positive!

Answers
Very positive b, c
Quite positive d, f
A little negative a
Very negative e

Exercise 5

Refer students to the *Key expressions*, and check the stress and intonation of the expressions. If necessary, model them and get the students to repeat them after you.

Students work in pairs, taking turns to use the six situations in the box to make suggestions, and respond, using the *Key expressions*. Model an example with a strong student.

Give feedback specifically on the phrases for making and responding to suggestions, using appropriate intonation.

Further practice
If students need more practice, go to *Practice file 15* on page 134 of the *Student's Book*.

Exercise 6
Students work in pairs. They will be considering ways to improve company motivation.

Refer them again to the *Key expressions*. Then ask the students to work in AB pairs, and to read the relevant information. Check they understand *bonus*.

When giving feedback, focus on accurate use of phrases from the *Key expressions*.

PRE-WORK LEARNERS Students could think about a company they know well, or consider how to improve staff motivation at the college where they are studying.

> **EXTRA ACTIVITY**
> For quick revision here, or at the beginning of next lesson, put a few ideas/suggestions on slips of paper. (These could be work-related, or not, depending on your students, e.g. 'Let's meet up on Saturday at 11 for an extra hour of English!', or 'What about keeping in touch between classes on email, in English!', or 'What about having a dress-down Friday, when everyone can wear jeans to work?') Ask the students to stand up in two lines, in two teams. Give the first person in each team a suggestion each, and ask them to read it out to the second person in the line: that person responds negatively (but politely!) and adds an alternative suggestion. The third student responds in the same way, and so on, down the line. Encourage students to use a range of phrases from the *Key expressions*.

Photocopiable worksheet
Download and photocopy *Unit 15 Business communication worksheet* from the teacher resources in the *Online practice*.

Talking point

The objective of this game is to practise the language and skills which the students have learnt in this book. You may wish to ask students to revise this before they start the game.

Students read the rules. Check they are familiar with 'heads' and 'tails' when using a coin. Emphasize that the aim of the game is to review language and skills from the book.

You will probably find that students complete the tasks in the squares reasonably well, but without necessarily using the language from this book. In these cases, it is up to you whether you insist on them doing so, perhaps by looking it up in the second copy of the *Student's Book* as suggested.

As they play, monitor and help with vocabulary queries.

For feedback, you could keep a 'hot card' for each student or pair. As they play, write down errors on their hot card, and at the end, give them their hot card for discussion and correction. If you have a large class, ask students to monitor each other's mistakes, and fix a penalty of 'two squares back' for anybody who makes a mistake. If students disagree, for example about correct pronunciation, they ask you to decide.

Give feedback on their ideas, as well as on accurate language use.

Progress test
Download and photocopy *Unit 15 Progress test* and *Speaking test* from the teacher resources in the *Online practice*.

Viewpoint 5

Preview

The topic of this *Viewpoint* is *A successful partnership*. In this *Viewpoint*, students first watch people talking about the type of company they work for. They then watch a video with Colin Goepfert, the Learning and Development Coach at John Lewis. Finally, they discuss how they could introduce a partnership scheme, similar to that at John Lewis, into their company.

Exercise 1

Students first match the types of companies to their definitions.

Find out if any of your students works for one of these company types.

Answers
1 c **2** a **3** d **4** b

Exercise 2

Students work in pairs and think of an example of each company type. Discuss some of their ideas as a group.

Exercise 3

▶ 01 Students read the first column in the table, and then watch the video. They should make notes about what each speaker says. If necessary, play the video again, pausing after each speaker.

Note that each speaker answers the first question and then answers about both the advantages and disadvantages.

Ask students if any of the speakers' comments or opinions are similar to their own. Discuss answers as a class.

Answers

	Speaker 1 (Lisa)	Speaker 2 (Sarah)	Speaker 3 (Timi)
Type of company	Sole trader	Public company	NGO (Non-Governmental Organization) / Charity
Advantages	Doesn't have to answer to anyone else – she has full control.	Held to a higher standard - have to be careful with revenue, investments, expenses to ensure growth of stock value.	Being able to make a difference to people around the world.
Disadvantages	Only her that is responsible for this company.	Difficult to think long term. Decision making is sometimes compromised.	Difficult to get other people to understand why helping other people is important.

Exercise 4

Students discuss what type of company they work for, and consider whether the advantages and disadvantages mentioned in **3** are true for their company.

PRE-WORK LEARNERS Ask students to think of a company they know well, decide what sort of company it is, and think about what its disadvantages or advantages may be.

EXTENSION Strong students could be asked to think about other advantages and disadvantages.

Exercise 5

Ask students to match the words and phrases in bold in sentences 1–7 to definitions a–g. Do the first one together.

Students check their answers with a partner, then check with the whole class.

Answers
1 d **2** e **3** c **4** f **5** g **6** a **7** b

Exercise 6

▶ 02 Before playing the video, ask students to look at the slides. Then play the video again for students to order them as they watch.

Students check their answers with a partner, and then check the answers together.

You may want to deal with any vocabulary students bring up, e.g. *in the region of* means approximately (and is not geographical). Other vocabulary that they may not be familiar with: *profit, proportion, annual pay, shareholder, dividend, bonus, market rate.*

Answers
A 3 **B** 4 **C** 1 **D** 2

VIDEO SCRIPT

(The John Lewis Partnership is one of the UK's leading retail businesses. Colin Goepfert is the Learning and Development Coach at John Lewis.)

The John Lewis Partnership came into being in 1950. We've now got in the region of 78,000 people who work in the John Lewis Partnership. It includes about 32 department stores up and down the country, over 250 Waitrose supermarkets plus our Internet business. We have a production unit up in Lancashire, near Blackburn, and also we have a farm of about 4,000 acres in Hampshire where we grow and produce a lot of the milk and apples and mushrooms that we sell in our Waitrose supermarket. We have partners, essentially most other businesses would refer to them as employees or staff, we call them partners because they are all partners in the true sense of the word. They all have responsibilities and share in the benefits of our business. That doesn't mean when they join us on day one they get one share of John Lewis, it means at the end of the year, when we've worked out our profit for that year, every partner would receive a proportion of their annual pay as a percentage. So whether you're a Saturday-only partner or the Chairman, you would all receive the same per cent of your pay as your bonus, so that's almost like the dividend that you would get if you were a shareholder in other business. We call them partners because they all have a part to play in our success and sharing that.

Like any business, we have to be successful and therefore we have to make a profit. Because we don't have any external shareholders we don't have to produce a dividend to keep other people happy. We have to make the profit and we want the profit to be sufficient to enable us to continue doing what we do. And what we do is to look after our partners in the terms of the employment and the benefits we offer, because we believe that if you look after the partners, they will therefore look after the customers; look after the customers, they will look after your profit, and we have what we call the partner-customer-profit cycle and that's what we live and work to.

Other ways that we kind of measure our success, obviously, is turnover, because the turnover feeds directly into the bonus, but we also look at the feedback we receive from outside bodies – *Which* reports, *Verdict* reports, the customer service groups that are available – and we regularly, between John Lewis and Waitrose, feature in the top two or three companies for those, again for us really important.

We like to always pay the best rate for the right level of performance. We're constantly looking at the, at what we call the market rate, which is what the going rate for a particular job is, but within our pay structure every partner has the opportunity to work their way up.

We have a very comprehensive training package called *Horizons*, which has a huge amount of resources, courses, books, videos, DVDs, coaching sessions that partners can sign up for to help them achieve the best in their performance. We have the bonus that we've mentioned earlier which was last year about 18%.

We also have in all of our workplaces subsidized dining, a minimum of four weeks' paid holiday rising to six weeks after ten years, we have a final salary non-contributory pension scheme. We offer something called long leave – after 25 years of continual service a partner can actually take six months off, fully paid, to just go and get away from their normal work regime and just experience something different.

So we're constantly trying to find new ways of making the life of our partners fuller and enable them to do more than they perhaps would do. Pay's important, but to us, pay is just one part of partner development and partner growth, and we hopefully have a pack that's second to none.

Exercise 7

Students work alone to match the titles 1–4 to the slides in **6**.

Students check their answers with a partner, and then check with the group.

Answers
1 C   2 D   3 A   4 B

Exercise 8

▶ 02 Before playing the video again, ask students to read the questions. Stronger students could try to answer them before they watch. Then play the video again. If necessary, pause the video after the information is mentioned.

Students check their answers with a partner. Then check the answers together.

Answers
2 Yes
3 Yes
4 No
5 Don't know
6 Don't know
7 Yes
8 No

Exercise 9

Students read the three options, and then tick the one that is closest to their own opinion. They then compare their ideas with a partner, giving reasons. Discuss some of their opinions with reasons as a whole class.

Exercise 10

Students could work with a different partner for these last two exercises. They are going to discuss introducing a similar partnership scheme for their own company. Give them time to read the three points. They should then discuss, and take notes on their answers and ideas. You could also encourage students to adapt the scheme if they have others ideas they think would work, e.g. about training or taking time off.

Monitor students as they work, and help if needed. Remind them to consider how they will measure success and calculate bonuses.

PRE-WORK LEARNERS   Students could think of a company they know well, and discuss how the John Lewis scheme (or a similar partnership scheme) could work. They could think about a company where friends or family work.

Exercise 11

Students work together to give the presentation. One student could present the overall plan (first point), while the other explains the employee benefits and how they will measure success.

Encourage others in the group to ask questions for clarification.

When they have all finished, vote on the best scheme. You could come up with your own criteria, or suggest giving points based on how easy it would be to implement, how the employees will benefit, and/or how easy it will be to measure success.

Further video ideas

You can find a list of suggested ideas for how to use video in the class in the teacher resources in the *Online practice*.

Practice file answer key

Unit 1

Working with words

Exercise 1
2 f 3 b 4 e 5 c 6 a

Exercise 2
2 based 6 products
3 operate 7 produce
4 subsidiaries 8 competitors
5 employees

Exercise 3
2 exporter 7 provide
3 subsidiaries 8 operates
4 products 9 services
5 based 10 produce
6 specialize

Business communication

Exercise 1
2 What (d) 3 Where (f) 4 Who (c)
5 What (a) 6 Why (b)

Exercise 2
2 i 3 a 4 e 5 c 6 g 7 b 8 d
9 f

Language at work

Exercise 1
2 is 7 have
3 specialize 8 specializes
4 starts 9 are
5 works 10 work
6 start

Exercise 2
b does 5 e do 10 i does 4
c Do you f are 9 j does 8
 have 7 g does 1
d is 2 h arrive 6

Exercise 3
2 don't 3 does 4 doesn't, does
5 aren't 6 don't

Unit 2

Working with words

Exercise 1
2 supplier 5 staff
3 employment 6 consultant
 agency 7 client
4 customers

Exercise 2
2 train 5 organizer
3 products 6 supply
4 calculate 7 consultation

Exercise 3
2 e 3 a 4 b 5 c

Business communication

Exercise 1
2 calling 7 back
3 This 8 Does
4 afraid 9 give
5 take 10 help
6 ask

Exercise 2
2 speaking 6 phoning
3 leave 7 calling
4 do 8 You're welcome
5 about 9 Speak

Language at work

Exercise 1
2 Is he staying 5 are those German
3 You aren't / You're engineers visiting
 not listening 6 She isn't working
4 I'm leaving

Exercise 2
2 a 3 b 4 f 5 d 6 e

Exercise 3
2 have 6 are becoming
3 work 7 are opening
4 are looking 8 get
5 buy 9 are trying

Unit 3

Working with words

Exercise 1
2 helpful 7 pretty
3 user 8 popular
4 quality 9 original
5 reliable 10 extremely
6 value

Exercise 2
2 phone 3 value 4 reliable
5 money 6 quality

Business communication

Exercise 1
Order of sentences: 1 5 7 4 8 6 3 9 2

Exercise 2
2 We wanted 6 Finally
3 We did this by 7 showed
4 First 8 the majority
5 Then we asked 9 we recommend

Language at work

Exercise 1
2 studied 8 called
3 built 9 didn't publish
4 had 10 started
5 became 11 made
6 spent 12 created
7 wrote

Exercise 2
2 did you have 5 did they stay
 lunch 6 did she join
3 did you see 7 did you spend
4 did Raul leave 8 did you send

Exercise 3
1 was 4 don't, decided
2 works, came 5 didn't, speaks
3 wasn't, didn't 6 doesn't, was

Unit 4

Working with words

Exercise 1
2 c 3 g 4 e 5 f 6 h 7 j 8 a
9 b 10 i

Exercise 2
2 of 3 to 4 for 5 with

Business communication

Exercise 1
2 g 3 b 4 h 5 a 6 e 7 c 8 f

Exercise 2
Across:
3 have 6 appointment 8 late
Down:
2 inviting 3 help 4 else 5 way
7 nice

Language at work

Exercise 1
2 b 3 b 4 a 5 b 6 a 7 b 8 a
9 b 10 b

Exercise 2
2 When did the company start?
3 How many people does the company
 employ?
4 Do you have a lot of competitors in the
 USA?
5 How much chewing gum do Americans
 eat?
6 Who are your main customers?

Unit 5

Working with words

Exercise 1
2 d 3 a 4 c 5 f 6 b

Exercise 2
2 report a problem
3 offer a solution
4 make a complaint
5 response times
6 get feedback

Exercise 3
2 query 3 discount 4 replacement
5 issue 6 credit voucher

Business communication

Exercise 1
Sentence order: 5 6 8 4 1 10 3 7 9 2

Exercise 2
2 I'm not very happy
3 I'm sorry
4 I'm afraid
5 we can offer you
6 check
7 sorry for
8 I'll deal with

Language at work

Exercise 1
2 more profitable
3 newest
4 nearer
5 most popular
6 more professional
7 worst
8 biggest
9 better

Exercise 2
2 T
3 F. It's the easiest to use.
4 T
5 F. It offers slower delivery than Arriba.
6 T
7 F. It's the least popular.
8 F. It's easier to use than Teslo's.

Unit 6

Working with words

Exercise 1
2 advertised
3 experience
4 qualification
5 skills
6 candidate
7 interview
8 reference

Exercise 2
2 qualified
3 recruitment
4 shortlist
5 skilled
6 advert/ advertisement
7 experienced
8 interviewed

Business communication

Exercise 1
2 issue 3 expensive 4 go
5 Another 6 suitable 7 sure

Exercise 2
2 One key advantage
3 I like the idea that
4 I'm not sure
5 another issue is
6 I'd go for
7 it's preferable
8 are more suitable

Language at work

Exercise 1
2 have told
3 have not / haven't found
4 has become
5 has / 's been
6 have left
7 have not / haven't recruited
8 have / 've asked
9 has / 's said
10 have / 've lost
11 have not / haven't had
12 have not / haven't made

Exercise 2
2 Have you h
3 Have you ever b
4 Did you have d
5 Has c
6 Did g
7 been a
8 did you send e

Unit 7

Working with words

Exercise 1
2 hand baggage
3 delayed flights
4 self-service check-in
5 weight restrictions
6 security scan
7 airline charges
8 baggage allowances
9 seat upgrade
10 missed connection

Exercise 2
2 extra 3 middle 4 cancelled 5 free
6 excess

Business communication

Exercise 1
2 c 3 a 4 h 5 d 6 b 7 f 8 e
9 j 10 i

Exercise 2
2 Would
3 Sorry
4 free
5 suits
6 Does
7 afraid
8 what
9 fine
10 shall
11 that's

Language at work

Exercise 1
2 she's going to
3 aren't going
4 I'm going to
5 he's visiting
6 I'll be
7 I'm going to
8 She's playing
9 won't be
10 'm meeting

Exercise 2
2 she's visiting
3 We're not having / We're not going to have
4 I'm meeting
5 I'll ask
6 I'm going to call / I'll call
7 I'll check
8 he isn't going to accept
9 I'll give
10 are starting / are going to start

Unit 8

Working with words

Exercise 1
2 process/ship
3 check/guarantee
4 shipment/order
5 ship/deliver
6 enquire about/ check
7 orders/goods

Exercise 2
Across:
4 place 8 ordered 9 guarantee
10 track
Down:
1 deliver 3 process 5 check
6 enquire 7 quoted

Business communication

Exercise 1
2 b 3 h 4 g 5 c 6 a 7 d 8 f

Exercise 2
2 could
3 show
4 of course
5 ask
6 mind
7 go ahead
8 just
9 sorry
10 Would

Language at work

Exercise 1
2 The invoice **was** sent yesterday.
3 Over a thousand guests **were** invited to the event.
4 The post **is collected** at 10 a.m. every day.
5 The software **is written / was written** by our engineers.
6 The meeting was **cancelled** because of the strike.

Exercise 2
2 is given/was given/will be given
3 were asked
4 are processed
5 are held
6 was installed
7 was delivered
8 is published

Exercise 3
2 An email was sent to all employees by the HR department.
3 The money was stolen (by someone).
4 The staff were informed about the decision (by the heads of department).

5 Salaries are discussed with employees individually.
6 The key to the safe is kept in his desk.

Unit 9

Working with words

Exercise 1
2 target audience
3 advertising campaign
4 new business
5 word of mouth
6 free publicity

Exercise 2
2 offer 3 conduct 4 increase 5 boost
6 reach

Exercise 3
2 search engines
3 advertising boards
4 targeted emails
5 promotional events

Business communication

Exercise 1
2 c 3 a 4 b 5 f 6 h 7 i 8 j
9 e 10 g

Exercise 2
2 I didn't catch that
3 I'm not with you
4 Could you be more specific
5 what was the time of the meeting
6 we're getting off the subject
7 we can come back to that later
8 we've covered everything
9 Can we move on to the next point
10 can we sum up what we've agreed

Language at work

Exercise 1
Students' own answers.

Exercise 2
2 Do I have/Do I need
3 has to/needs to, are allowed
4 Am I allowed
5 need to/have to
6 can, aren't allowed
7 don't have, can't

Unit 10

Working with words

Exercise 1
2 g 3 e 4 h 5 a 6 b 7 c 8 f

Exercise 2
2 carbon emissions
3 Global warming
4 fossil fuels
5 energy consumption
6 reduce pollution
7 eco-friendly
8 throw away

Exercise 3
1 pollution, consumption
2 glass, plastic, newspapers
3 petrol, less water, electricity
4 the environment, cities, rivers

Business communication

Exercise 1
2 I'm here today
3 I'll come
4 let's start with
5 My next point
6 lastly
7 to sum up
8 that brings me
9 Thanks very much
10 As I said before

Exercise 2
2 start 3 overview 4 look 5 Then
6 finally 7 all 8 tell

Language at work

Exercise 1
2 agree, 'll have
3 will he say, asks
4 don't improve, 'll lose
5 won't accept, doesn't know
6 don't print, 'll use
7 'll use, leave
8 won't pay, waits
9 will it take, go
10 don't decrease, will continue

Exercise 2
3 will it cost
4 decide
5 don't sell
6 'll save
7 will consume
8 do
9 won't be
10 drive
11 look
12 'll see
13 will increase
14 rises

Unit 11

Working with words

Exercise 1
2 venue 3 guests 4 budget
5 host company 6 package

Exercise 2
2 had 3 arranged 4 entertains
5 booked 6 accept

Exercise 3
2 host company
3 entertain
4 held
5 venue
6 accepted
7 budget
8 guests
9 book
10 arranged
11 had

Business communication

Exercise 1
2 Would you like to join us for lunch?
3 Shall I get you a ticket for the concert?
4 Thanks for asking, but I'm not free
5 Would you like me to book a table?
6 Would you like a glass of water?
7 Do you fancy going to the cinema?

Exercise 2
2 Would you like to take a break?
3 Do you fancy seeing a football game?
4 Shall I reserve a table?
5 Would you like to visit the new factory now?
6 Would you like me to meet you at the airport?

Exercise 3
2 Thanks for the 3 very good of
4 like me to 5 asking, but 6 be great

Language at work

Exercise 1
Countable: shop, reservation, hotel, event, person
Uncountable: information, money, entertainment, luggage, accommodation

Exercise 2
2 are
3 Are
4 many
5 some
6 Is
7 much
8 was
9 many

Exercise 3
2 an
3 Are
4 any
5 Is
6 a
7 some
8 much

Unit 12

Working with words

Exercise 1
2 f 3 h 4 a 5 g 6 c 7 b 8 d

Exercise 2
2 safety record, excellent
3 perform well, encouraging
4 satisfactory, socially responsible
5 poor, manage costs
6 environmental performance, average
7 good reputation, excellent
8 workplace diversity, disappointing

Business communication

Exercise 1
2 from 3 to 4 by 5 to 6 by 7 to

Exercise 2
2 rise
3 dropped
4 see
5 declined
6 remained stable
7 notice
8 risen
9 increasing

Exercise 3
Students' own answers

Language at work

Exercise 1
2 I've worked
3 for several years
4 I was
5 I developed
6 for four years
7 I left

Exercise 2
2 When did she join One Step Fitness?
3 How long was she Assistant Manager at One Step Fitness?
4 How long has she been a manager?
5 Where did she work from 2006 to 2010?
6 How long has she been responsible for sales growth?
7 How long did she work at Sun Sports Clothing?
8 How long has she been in the sports and fitness industry?

Unit 13

Working with words

Exercise 1
Across:
2 development 4 change
Down:
1 shortage 2 demand 3 threat
4 crisis 5 growth

Exercise 2
2 estimate 3 worse 4 forecasts
5 threatens 6 run

Business communication

Exercise 1
2 Do you think the situation will improve?
3 I hope we won't have to close the factory.
4 The staff will definitely support the decision.
5 Are the new rules likely to affect us?
6 Unemployment probably won't decrease before 2025.
7 We're unlikely to have more free time in the future.

Exercise 2
2 likely to find a substitute for oil
3 will probably be affected first
4 are likely to rise dramatically
5 definitely won't go up
6 Hopefully, we'll develop

Exercise 3
2 are 3 Hopefully 4 will 5 probably
6 likely

Language at work

Exercise 1
2 We'll finish the report today.
3 The manager may not / might not be in her office right now.
4 The secretary may/might know when the meeting is.
5 I won't get the job I applied for.
6 They may not / might not give us a pay rise this year.
7 He won't go on any more business trips.
8 The staff may/might be more motivated.

Exercise 2
2 'll be
3 won't feel
4 will exist
5 may/might lose
6 won't / may/ might not apply
7 won't find
8 will improve
9 might/may not be
10 might/may

Unit 14

Working with words

Exercise 1
2 h 3 b 4 d 5 c 6 a 7 e 8 g

Exercise 2
2 save
3 schedule
4 leave
5 spend
6 waste
7 leave
8 run
9 ahead
10 time

Business communication

Exercise 1
a 1 b 6 c 4 d 9 e 2 f 5 g 10
h 7 i 3 j 8

Exercise 2
2 Oh dear. What's the problem exactly?
3 Basically, I ordered 50 ducks but you sent me chickens.
4 I'm sorry. Would you agree to keep the chickens?
5 No, I'm afraid I couldn't accept that.
6 Would it be OK if we delivered the ducks today?
7 Yes, that would allow me to have them for the weekend.
8 OK, I'll send them today.

Language at work

Exercise 1
2 didn't know
3 would you think about
4 they would give
5 found themselves
6 they could start
7 might they do
8 could only read
9 we would recommend

Exercise 2
1 had
2 would, had
3 need, 'll
4 were, would
5 gave, might work
6 'll finish, works
7 wouldn't, didn't pay
8 Will, send
9 knew, 'd tell
10 don't, will be

Unit 15

Working with words

Exercise 1
2 e 3 f 4 b 5 d 6 h (or c)
7 c (or h) 8 a

Exercise 2
2 feedback
3 develop, skills
4 step back
5 set goals (or objectives)
6 motivate
7 achieve
8 improve

Exercise 3
2 motivate
3 feedback
4 develop/improve
5 skills
6 achieve
7 prospects

Business communication

Exercise 1
a 1 b 7 c 6 d 4 e 3 f 2 g 5
h 8

Exercise 2
2 Maybe we should set
3 How about asking
4 Shall we think
5 We could introduce
6 I suggest you/we discuss

Exercise 3
b sure, think 2
c let's 6
d might, don't 5
e question 3
f great, about 1

Language at work

Exercise 1
2 g shouldn't
3 e don't think
4 b could
5 a should
6 c mustn't
7 d must

Exercise 2
2 must
3 could
4 shouldn't
5 should
6 should
7 must
8 mustn't